A JOY FILLED LIFE

UNLOCKING THE KINGDOM IN YOUR LIFE

Joy E. Miller

A Joy Filled Life: Unlocking the Kingdom in Your Life

All other Scripture taken from the King James Version as noted.

ISBN-13: 978-0-9968715-6-3 Print edition
ISBN: 978-0-9968715-7-0 Ebook Edition

Printed in the United States of America

RevMedia Publishing
PO BOX 5172
Kingwood, TX 77325

A publishing division of Revelation Ministries
www.revmediapublishing.com

1 2 3 4 5 6 7 8 9 10 11 21 20 19 18 17 16 15 14

ABOUT THE AUTHOR

My personal library is full of books on all kinds of spiritual topics but none were about the overall culture of kingdom life. They touched individual topics, such as how to pray, how to have kingdom authority, how to walk in the Spirit. There were stories of people, places and things. When God revealed his assignment to me, I went back to my library and I could not find anything that was an overview of the kingdom principles which God wants us to base our lives on or how Jesus' life and death established a way to restore his kingdom principles. It was based on this idea that the book **A Joy Filled Life** was written.

My spiritual gift is a teacher and through-out life whether I was working in the corporate world, as a self-employed business owner or serving God, I have always used my teaching ability to teach others "lessons I have learned in life". I am the most fulfilled when I am teaching and so using these skills I wrote **A Joy Filled Life** to help both the mature Christian and the new believer understand the top fundamental principles Jesus taught us while on earth about his Kingdom. In order to have a life of joy, we must walk in these principles. I hope reviewing them will help you appreciate in a new deeper level what Jesus did to provide YOU a "life of joy".

Joy E. Miller

Follower of Jesus, Mother of 3, Grandmother of 14, Educator, Artist and Author

CONTENTS

"A Joy Filled Life"

All scripture references are quoted from **THE MESSAGE BIBLE**,
unless followed by **KJ** for the **KING JAMES BIBLE**.

Visit Joy at
www.ajoyfilledlife.org

INTRODUCTION

Kingdom of God

God is in the business of restoration. To "restore" means to bring back to the original status or to the perfect way that God intended something to be. As perfect as God is, he made humans perfect too; but today, man is not perfect nor is his universe. God being an all knowing God, knew that both man and the earth would become less than intended. God knew it would all have to be restored one day. His universe was made of three kingdoms:

- Heaven, the spiritual realm, serves as home for God and his heavenly creatures and includes his throne room
- Earth, the human realm, serves as man's home which includes the sky, land and seas
- Hell, the demonic realm, the home of Satan and his followers

Because of the fall of man through sin, the Kingdom of God "culture" had been tampered with. And ever since that point, God has been trying to restore it. How do we define culture? How do we fall short of living the "Kingdom Life" that God had intended us to enjoy?

Culture can be defined as a way of life formed by how we were trained and educated. It is affected by "our" local society's beliefs; therefore, we have different cultures as a result of the region we live in, family environment, educational level and spiritual training. Our culture affects our way of thinking and how we live our life.

God says: "I am going to restore kingdom culture in my church". If he said that, it means we are not living in the complete and perfect culture he had planned for us. I am of the "now" generation known as the "church age", and as I prayed about what God said, I realized I was only scratching the surface of "Kingdom of God Culture". His text book, The Holy Bible, provides us with the information we need and through the guidance of his Holy Spirit, we are being guided into "all knowledge and wisdom" of that culture. I don't want to settle for less than what my King, Jesus, died on the cross for me to have! Do you? So, what we need is a spiritual revelation of what God intended the Kingdom of God on earth to look like!

Becoming a Christian is only the first step to being restored in the kingdom. Over the years, so many things have affected my personal restoration: the church I attend, the people I listen to, and how much continual education I involve myself in. I realized the thing I needed most was to have the King Himself as my teacher. God, Jesus and the Holy Spirit are my "King", and to be restored into the fullness of his culture, I must spend more time in his classroom. I need to walk like him, talk like him, and think like him.

This type of transformation is not done in a moment of time, but in thousands of moments, in the presence of God. It is a lifestyle that we need to change. I had always considered myself a lifetime learner and had spent a good portion of time developing my spiritual life. However, this kind of transformation takes much more than just being willing to change. It requires an understanding and practice of utilizing the principles of the Kingdom of God.

I was saved in a small Baptist church at six years old. My family lived less than two blocks from the church. Both of my parents were Christians and they always encouraged me to attend church as much as I wanted. I was a three times a week church kid. As life progressed, there were times that I remained close to my spiritual roots and times that I was so involved with life that I put my spirituality on the back burner. But, God was never far from me and he continually drew me back to himself. By the time I was 30, my hunger for him was ravenous and I continually was searching for a deeper walk and studying his Word both in formal Bible studies and alone, saturating myself in his Word. As a result, I became a teacher, mentor and speaker for Jesus.

When the Spirit prompted me to write a book, I said, who am I, to write about spiritual topics and what would you want me to write about...hasn't everything been written? After months of fighting with the Spirit about it, God reminded me that obedience is much more important than all the sacrifices that I had made. "Just be obedient", was his answer to me. I finally submitted and started to try picking a subject, without any success. After days and days of writing, "small blurbs" on different topics were written. I finally heard in my spirit. All of these subjects are about the Kingdom of God that Jesus, Paul and the other disciples spoke about in the New Testament.

Then God, by his Spirit, showed me that the Bible was the story of how his creation was destroyed by sin and how he was going to restore his kingdom on earth back to his original concept. Most books touched individual areas, such as how to pray, how to have kingdom authority, how to walk in Spirit. Some books told the stories of people, places and things and interpreted them to fit into our daily life. Few books were about the overall culture of kingdom life he wants for us today.

God revealed to me that my assignment was to reveal his kingdom and it's principles that he desires his believers to walk in. With the charge given, I went back to my library and I could not find anything that was an overview of these kingdom principles. God wants us to base our lives on how Jesus' life and death established a new way to restore his kingdom principles. It was based on this idea that the book **A Joy Filled Life** was written.

For years, I just could not get my mind wrapped around what the Kingdom of God looked like...so I have attempted to give every Believer a beginning point, so they have a better picture of what God intends his kingdom on earth to look like. I believe that as I'm writing, God will stop me and say, "That's the picture of my kingdom I'm giving the church today!" And then, the next day he will continue to reveal more things that can be added. If we don't get the basic principles, how can we move on to the deeper principles? If we, as the citizens of the Kingdom, can get these activated in our lives, I'm sure God will have more for us. He is a "BIG" God and his kingdom goes on throughout eternity. So, I'm sure he will continue to take us to new places of understanding him and his principles.

I have written this book as the Spirit has led me; but in no way do I assume that every principle has been included. Each of these principles have had hundreds of books written about them, with much more details on the "how to's" than this book. I invite you to go deeper in the areas that the Spirit quickens to your spirit... areas you need to work or improve on. Personally, he has continued to quicken to me of my need to go deeper as I have written these truths.

Jesus has come to bring us abundant life; but we must understand it and we must fight for it. Hopefully this book will show you what Satan has stolen from you and incite you to reclaim it. In the Book of Revelation, John describes what happened like this:

"A Sign appeared in Heaven: a Woman dressed in sunlight, standing on the moon, and crowned with Twelve Stars.

She was giving birth to a Child and cried out in pain of childbirth.

And then another Sign alongside the first: a huge and fiery Dragon!

It had seven heads and ten horns, a crown on each of the seven heads. With one flick of its tail it knocked a third of the Stars from the sky and dumped them on Earth.

The Dragon crouched before the Woman in childbirth, poised to eat up the Child when it came.

The Women gave birth to a Son who will shepherd all nations with an iron rod. Her Son was seized and placed safely before God on his Throne.

The Woman herself escaped to the desert to a place of safety prepared by God, all comforts provided her for one thousand two hundred and sixty days.

War broke out in Heaven. Michael and his Angels fought the Dragon. The Dragon and his Angels fought back, but were no match for Michael. They were cleared out of Heaven, not a sign of them left.

The great Dragon—ancient Serpent, the one called Devil and Satan, the one who led the whole Earth astray—thrown out, and all his Angels thrown out with him, thrown down to Earth.

Then I heard a strong voice out of Heaven saying, salvation and power are established! Kingdom of our God, authority of his Messiah! The Accuser of our brothers and sisters thrown out, who accused them day and night before God.

They defeated him through the blood of the Lamb and the bold word of their witness. They weren't in love with themselves; they were willing to die for Christ.
So rejoice, O Heavens, and all who live there, but doom to Earth and sea, for the Devil's come down on you with both feet; he's had a great fall; he's wild and raging with anger; he hasn't much time and he knows it.
When the Dragon saw he had been thrown to Earth, he went after the Woman who had given birth to the Man-Child." Revelation 12: 1-13

We need a full revelation of all God has provided and to realize the end described in Revelation will happen. Jesus will return, a victorious King, and His kingdom, the Kingdom of God, will be restored!

This is the reason for the 'Battlefield' on earth.

God's job is to recover and restore!

Our job is to fight the 'Good Fight' and win all God has for us.

Joy Smothermon Miller – Soldier, Conqueror and Child of the King!

CHAPTER 1

Kingdom Vision

In my vision, I was sitting in my Chrysler 300 and everything was very peaceful. I was just enjoying the drive I was on, as the wind blew through my hair. I had no direction, no appointments, and no requirement of me. My job was just to sit back and enjoy the ride. Then I realized that the motor of the car was not even actually turned on and I was sitting there waiting for something to happen. It was like I was in some kind of holding pattern waiting my time for something to trigger so I could start a journey. It was dark and I couldn't see anything around me. I felt like I was in some kind of a capsule or cocoon, just sitting there waiting my turn for whatever was about to happen.

Then all of a sudden, the lights came on and I looked around me and realized my car was in something like a garage. It was metal and had curved convex walls and I could hear the wind outside of the building blowing very strong.

But nothing was happening inside the room. I was still just sitting in the car and waiting patiently for something to happen. It was so peaceful and I was not anxious of anything that might be going on. I was quite aware that behind the scenes something was happening and whatever it was, it was preventing me from the starting my journey.

It was kind of like sitting at the starting gate for the beginning of a great race or waiting in the seat of a roller coaster and not knowing when the ride would begin or what would happen on it.

All of a sudden, a large door was opening in front of me. Light was beginning to enter the room I was sitting in. It was entering from the top of a door - not a traditional door that swung open from the side, but one that was dropping open from the ceiling. The door was huge and was made of metal. The winds were rushing in. The noise from the metal door opening was cracking and popping because of size and weight of it. It took a few minutes for it to completely lower to what I thought would be a platform for me to drive out on but it continued to drop down and soon it dropped so low I could not see it any longer. Then I realized I was sitting on the edge of the opening and my front wheels had no surface to roll forward onto. I was on the edge of something and if anything unexpected happened, I could be in trouble.

As I looked around, I realized I was actually inside an airplane and the opening of the door exposed me to elements around the plane. It was a military plane, like they use to transport tanks and equipment to battlefields. The door that opened usually became the ramp so that they could drive the vehicles into the plane and load the supplies for the troops. The winds on the outside of the plane were picking up and getting stronger and was making a roaring sound in my ears and I realized the plane was not sitting on the runway but was actually flying.

All of a sudden something was behind my car and it was moving toward the car and before I knew what was happening, my car with me in it was being pushed out of the plane. The car and I were in free-fall and my heart started pounding and I grew anxious quickly for the first time.

I knew I was out of control and just for a moment, I tried to figure out how I could get control of the situation.

- I tried to start my car's engine, but nothing happened.
- I tried turning the steering wheel to see if I could control the direction, but nothing happened.
- I tried stomping on the brakes and the gas pedal, but nothing changed.
- I even tried the emergency brake, to no avail.

I was in a frenzy and out of control...free falling down, down toward the earth from the peaceful place inside my car into a chaotic situation, a situation out of my control. Nothing I did would stop the weight of the car being pulled to the ground by the force of gravity.

Finally I thought, "I can't do anything about this, so I might as well sit back and enjoy the ride."

As I rested my head against the head rest of the driver's seat, I opened my eyes just to see the view. It was at this time that I came out of my dream and realized I was awake and was now in an open vision and everything changed. Fear had left me and it was as if my senses were heightened and I was more interested in what I could see and the sensations of the experience I was now in. Peace had returned to me and I knew God had something to show me.

I looked out the front window of the car and could see the topography of the land. In the distance was a mountain range popping out of the flat desert land below me. It was like a picture I've always wanted to paint of West Texas, where everything was so flat before me that the distance to the mountain wasn't measurable and seemed to go on forever. Whether it was 10 miles or 100, I could not decide for there was nothing along the way for reference.

As I looked across the horizon, my eyes caught sight of a road coming out of the mountains. And on the road, was a car moving at what I thought was a very fast speed. Again, I had no reference of distance or speed of the car.

I just fixed my eyes on the car. It was so far away and so tiny that finally my eyes got bored and I started looking around at the landscape. It was so beautiful! The light was behind me and was just beginning to touch the top of the range of mountains. I could see features of things that I had not been able to see before and I became enthralled with God's beautiful creation. My artistic creative mind wanted to take everything in so I could later paint this once in a lifetime experience.

After an unknown time, I looked again at the road and the car traveling on it. It seemed to be moving faster as it got closer to my fall line. I traced it for mile after mile coming straight toward me. All of a sudden, I wondered if it was going to intersect my path of free fall.

As I finally looked right below me, I saw a spot with a large "X" in a circle on the pavement below me. It was apparent that God was showing me where I would land.

Time was starting to move so fast and yet time was allowing me to enjoy the ride of my life. I knew there would be an end to the ride but I had been allowed to enjoy this amazing journey. The craziness of me trying to control the ride before I crashed and ended in a heap of nothingness at the "X" had dissipated. The peace I experienced allowed me to enjoy the free-fall and the slowing down of time allowed me to see the landscape with crystal clarity.

I looked at the "X" once more and I looked on the horizon for the car. There it was - still on the road and heading toward me at an ever-growing rapid speed! I remember looking back and forth at the car and "X" and then I would look at the

"X" and where the car was on the highway. Back and forth my eyes travelled, trying to figure out once again what was going to happen. I began to calculate my rate of free fall and the car's rate of speed to determine whether we were going to collide and hit the "X" at the same time.

I then calmly began to pray, "God, don't let me crash with the car – don't let the weight of my car hit an innocent person driving down the road. This situation that I am in should not cause the death of others that are just driving along minding their own business. "

My eyes kept going back and forth from the car on the road to the "X" and from the "X" to my car falling through the atmosphere. Back and forth, back and forth. "Please God, don't let innocent people get hurt!" was my cry to God.

Time stood still, yet time was flying now, all at the same time. Until, in a split second, at the last moment before my car hit the car on the road, the person driving the car must have seen my car falling and started to calculate what was going to happen too. At the last moment, before we could collide, the driver took control of the situation to stop our collision. He made a choice to hit the gas pedal of his car. The increase in speed corrected what would have ended in a terrible disaster. He saved himself and others that might have been in his car with him. By hitting the accelerator, in a moment, his car took off like a rocket and had moved pass the point of collision, as my car hit the ground right at the "X".

At that moment, I remember coming out of the vision and I started thanking God for not letting me hit the car and destroying everyone in it. I was so happy and joyful for what I thought was godly intervention. Then in the middle of my praise, I was in the present and wide awake when I heard a voice in my spirit saying...

> "Joy, you **missed** it again. My ways are higher than your ways. My plans for you are bigger and better than any you may have for yourself or those around you.
>
> You **missed** it again! You missed my perfect will for you and for the other person.
>
> It was my will that you both hit the "X" at the same time. **My ways and my will are prefect."**

Even when we think we know what is best for us and when things seem like the only good way for something to be, if it is not God's way or his will, we lose. It must be the "Kingdom Way" to attain God's best for us.

What is the "Kingdom's Way"?

What did God mean when he said, "My ways and my will are perfect." It is only when we study God's Word and submit to him, that we can comprehend his ways and his will. To recognize the "Kingdom Way", we must understand what a kingdom looks like, what makes up a kingdom and what makes one kingdom different from another. Every kingdom has a city where the King lives and governs his people. In the Kingdom of God, Jerusalem is the earthly city that God has chosen for headquarters and from his viewpoint, it is the center of his kingdom on the earth. Let's explore a kingdom and a *"City, with real eternal foundations—the City designed and built by God." Hebrew 11:10.*

Every kingdom has one purpose; it is the King's domain. Picture God's kingdom as you read Psalms 47.

> *"Applause, everyone, Bravo, bravissimo! Shout God-songs at the top of your lungs! GOD Most High is stunning, astride land and ocean (earth). He crushes hostile people, puts nations at our feet. He set us at the head of the line, prize-winning Jacob, his favorite. Lord cheers as God climbs the mountain, a ram's horn blast at the summit. Sing songs to God, sing out! Sing praises to God, sing praises: sing praises unto our King, sing praises. He's Lord over earth, so sing your best songs to God. God is Lord of godless nations—sovereign, he's King of the mountain. Princes from all over are gathered, people of Abraham's God. The power of earth are God's—he soars over all."*

He has unlimited power and he has absolute power to rule over his subjects that are born in his territory and live in his kingdom.

Who qualifies to be God's subjects?

Those who are born again...

- One of Jesus' followers said to him, *"Rabbi, we all know you're a teacher straight from God. No one could do all the God-pointing, God-revealing acts you do if God weren't in on it. Jesus said, "You're absolutely right. Take it from me: Unless a person is born from above, it's not possible to see what I'm pointing to—to God's kingdom." John 3:3*

Those who trusted in his Son, Jesus, who rescued them from the Devil...

- *Thanking the Father (OUR KING) who makes us strong enough to take part in everything bright and beautiful that He has for us. God rescued us from dead-end alleys and dark dungeons. He set us up in the kingdom of the Son He loves so much, the Son who got us out of the pit we were in, got rid of the sins we were doomed to keep repeating. In whom we have redemption through his blood, even the forgiveness of sins. We look at this Son and see the God who cannot be seen. We look at this Son and see God's original purpose in everything created. For everything, absolutely everything, above and below, visible and invisible, rank after rank after rank of angels—everything got started in him and finds it purpose in him. He was there before any of it came into existence and holds it all together right up to this moment. And when it comes to the church, he organizes and holds it together, like a head does a body. He was supreme in the beginning and—leading the resurrection parade—he is supreme in the end.*

  From beginning to end he's there, towering far above everything, everyone. So spacious is he, so roomy, that everything of God finds it proper place in him without crowding. Not only that, but all the broken and dislocated pieces of the universe—people and things, animals and atoms—get properly fixed and fit together in vibrant harmonies, all because of his death, his blood that poured down from the Cross. You yourselves are a case study of what he does. At one time you all had your backs turned to God, thinking rebellious thoughts of him, giving him trouble every chance you got. But now, by giving himself completely at the Cross, actually dying for you, Christ brought you over to God's side and put your lives together, whole and holy in his presence. You don't walk away from a gift like that! You stay grounded and steady in that bond of trust, constantly tuned in to the Message, careful not to be distracted or diverted. There is no other Message—just this one. Every creature under heaven gets this same Message. Colossians 1:12-23

Those who submit themselves as a sacrifice to God, for service in the kingdom...

- *"Present yourselves as building stones for the construction of a sanctuary vibrant with life, in which you'll serve as holy priest offering Christ-approved lives up to God. 1 Peter 2:5-6*

Those who want to be discipled by Jesus...

- *"When Jesus saw his ministry drawing huge crowds, he climbed a hillside. Those who were apprenticed to him, the committed climbed with him. Arriving at a quiet place, he sat down and taught his climbing companions." Matthew 5:1*

And those who accept Jesus as the gate will enter the kingdom...

"Jesus told a simple story, but they had no idea what he was talking about. So he tried again. "I'll be explicit, then. I am the Gate for the sheep. All those others are up to no good—sheep stealers, every one of them. But the sheep didn't listen to them. I am the Gate. Anyone who goes through me will be cared for—will freely go in and out, and find pasture." (Parable of the voice of the Shepherd) John 10:6-9

"Jesus is 'the stone you masons threw out, which is now the cornerstone.' Salvation comes no other way; no other name has been or will be given to us by which we can be saved, only this one." Acts 4:12

Those who accept Jesus cannot live as subjects in two kingdoms. As born-again Christians, they are no longer subjects of the kingdom of Satan but now reside in the Kingdom of God...

- The process of salvation begins with justification through Jesus. This commences the education process of learning the principles of their new kingdom and learning the characteristics of their King...Jesus. The new residents of the kingdom begin to see the multi-facets of his personality and benefits of his kingdom.

- The process of sanctification also starts, when the believer begins to take on the godly characteristics of their King. They grow from glory to glory to become holy like he is holy.
    1. *Jesus said, "I'm telling you, once and for all, that unless you return to square one and start over like children, you're not even going to get a look at the kingdom, let alone get in."* *Matthew 18:3*
    2. *"So here's what I want you to do, God helping you: Take your everyday, ordinary life—your sleeping, eating, going to work and walking-around life—and place it before God as an offering. Embracing what God does for you is the best thing you can do for Him."* *Romans 12:1-2*
    3. *"You love the right and hate the wrong. And that is why God, your very own God, poured fragrant oil on your head, marking you out as king from among your dear companions."* *Psalms 45:7*

At this point, everything around and within the Christian begins to change. They begin to conform to their new kingdom culture. Their beliefs and customs, their way of thinking, behaving and working are the complete opposite to their old life. New Christians have new attitudes, values and goals. This is the "Kingdom Way" and they are now experiencing "kingdom living".

These are the things that will be discovered and studied in "**A Joy Filled Life**" as you learn kingdom principles. Many have walked this road before you and many will follow you through these same transformation passages that you will experience. Some of the principles you may have mastered, while others you are presently learning the processes and techniques. Still other principles you may have only heard about and have never walked in. Each person will be at a different place in their journey, but it is for sure that all will reach their destination...the complete revelation of the Kingdom of God and all that God has put in place for those that love him and are willing to sacrifice their earthly life for an eternal home in his perfect kingdom.

The Vision that I told in the beginning of the chapter will be reviewed again at the end of the book. I pray that after this study of the kingdom, your interpretation of the Vision will be much more revealing of what all God provides for his children (subjects) and how much deeper His love is for those who decide to follow his principles and live joyfully in his kingdom.

Kingdom Thinking

What is the difference in a dream and a vision?

Have you ever experienced a God given vision? If so, describe the experience.

What was the purpose of the "Vision"? Did you get the interpretation of the vision immediately?

What is a parable? Explain the how visions and dreams can have the same purposes?

Describe what is your definition of a kingdom?

Use the description of an Earthly Kingdom to define the Kingdom of God?

Describe God's requirements for a person to become a subject in his kingdom.

The picture, "Crossing Over", can represents one of the many crossings over in your life. Can you relate "Your Salvation" as a crossing over and why?

Keys to the Kingdom

- In the Kingdom of God, Jerusalem is the earthly city that God has chosen for headquarters and from his viewpoint, it is the center of his kingdom on the earth.
- God has unlimited power and he has absolute power to rule over his subjects that are born in his territory and live in his kingdom.
- Jesus is the gate which we must go through in order to enter the Kingdom of God.
- Only those who accept Jesus can be subjects in the Kingdom of God.
- Once a person lives in God's kingdom, the process of sanctification begins. His subjects begin to take on the godly characteristics of their King, Jesus. They grow from glory to glory to become holy like he is holy.
- A complete revelation of the Kingdom of God and all that God has put in place for those that love him results in, his subjects through their willingness to sacrifice their earthly life for an eternal home in his perfect kingdom.

Crossing Over

by Joy E. Miller

"Crossing Over" was painted to remind us of all the crossing overs we do in our lifetime.

The couple in the picture is at the halfway point of the bridge. They are at the point of moving forward, to complete the crossing, or turning back -never to see what awaits beyond the waterfall. Throughout our lives, one phase of life leads us to face new challenges and new levels of growth. With each "Crossing Over", take with you the memories of the past, and move forward with new Hopes and Dreams of what the future will bring.

CHAPTER 2

Kingdom of God vs Kingdom of Satan

How many times have we missed something good because we didn't understand what or how God thinks?

The Kingdom of God is like that. We accept Jesus as our Savior and expect everything to go along as if nothing has changed. Salvation is not business as usual. How could it be the same when we now live in a new kingdom with all the privileges and challenges that come with it?

We first need to know what the Kingdom of God means. Most of the time, people do not even slow down to consider what has changed or how it is different than our old earthly kingdom. No matter how old we are, life when we become a Christian completely changes – it doesn't matter if we are a child, adolescent, young adult, adult or mature senior citizen. We don't even stop and consider that we live in the same house, have the same family, friends and job, but we have been transformed anew. So what has changed? In reality, everything in our spirit has changed. Our desires and spiritual goals have been awakened in us. And we have moved from living in the kingdom of this world ruled by Satan to the Kingdom of God ruled by the God of the Universe.

I was a child when I accepted Jesus as my Savior and I am so thankful that it happened when I was so young. My life had not been tainted by the sins of the earthly kingdom. It did not appear that much had changed; however, my whole future had just changed courses. The event seemed small but in retrospect, it was major. I knew that Jesus had saved me but did I really realize that Jesus would continually save me over and over again from the kingdom of Darkness to the kingdom of Light (Kingdom of God).

I really was saved from so many evil things; because of my young age, my heart's desire was always to please God and do what he considered to be the right thing. Being raised in a Christian home with Christian parents was such a blessing. Those early years were filled with putting godly things in my spirit for my future. I was always surrounded with good people trying to do the same. That is not to say I did not sin or make mistakes, but there wasn't the exposure to ungodly things that would make my decisions harder for me. However, I did live in God's kingdom, but I also lived on the earth with the influences of the kingdom of Satan and how they would affect me as I grew up.

As I matured into adulthood my mind began questioning these earthly principles. And like so many other young people, I became rebellious wanting to experience what the earthly kingdom offered. Satan, at the same time, became like a 'Roaring Lion' tempting me to try the things of his kingdom. The Bible warns us to *"Be sober, be vigilant, because your adversary the devil, as a roaring lion, walked about, seeking whom he may devour." 1 Peter5:8 KJ*

And before long, I began to learn that the two kingdoms are in conflict with each other. In fact, they are the opposite of each other. Let's take a look at the two kingdoms and see how they contrast.

KINGDOM OF EARTH /GOD	**KINGDOM OF THIS WORLD/SATAN**
King – God (Old T) Jesus (New T)	Satan
Children of God our Father	Children of Satan
Motivated by love and honor	Motivated by fear
Kingdom of Light	Kingdom of Darkness
Everything leads to eternal life	Everything leads to death
Changes our life from the inside (spirit) out	Changes your life by doing things, works, methods
Desires Relationship with followers	Desires Religious works
Citizen of Heaven, living on earth	Citizen of Hell, living on earth
Helpers - Ministering angels	Helpers - Demons
Economic System – money works for the citizens and they have access to heaven's economy. No limits- "give and it will be given to you"	Economic System – limited to the world's economy. Limited by their paycheck or corrupt activities
Citizens rule over everything on the earth	Citizens ruled by passions, possessions and lust

Love your enemies, bless those who bless you, do good to those who hate you and pray for them who spitefully use you	Retaliate, sue, and attack those who persecute or mistreat you
Lay down your life for others	Self-defense, self-image, self-reliance, self-respect
Able to bring unseen things into the seen world by faith, working by love	Able to bring unseen things into the seen world by faith, working in fear
Healthcare system – by Jesus' stripes we are healed	Healthcare system – limited to doctors, medicine and insurance
Revelation knowledge from God in addition to natural senses	Head knowledge in addition to natural senses
Humble yourself	Promote yourself
The merciful shall obtain mercy	Show no mercy, dog-eat-dog, take no prisoners
Pray to do the will of God on earth as it is in heaven	Do your own thing, live life as you please
Bible is standard of living, tells us what is permitted	Everyone does what is right in their own sight
God's name is holy	God's name is slandered
Hate what God hates. Love what God loves	Call evil good and good evil

** Limited list of differences – add your own to list!*

Our journey on earth is to discover which kingdom we want to reside in. The quality of our life depends on our choice. And then we must grow into maturity of that kingdom. If we choose the Kingdom of God, our job is not to explore the kingdom of this world but to understand all the principles and benefits of the Kingdom of God. (Any discussion of the kingdom of this world is only to understand how it relates to and affects the Kingdom of God.)

Origination of the Kingdom of God (Heaven and Earth) for Us Today

"In the beginning God created the heaven and the earth."

This is the first sentence in the King James Bible (most people's first Bible). The Bible opens with one of the most all-encompassing statement in man's history. Books by theologians and scientist have been written on the subject of the creation of the world and development of humanity. Today, we still don't know what all God included and excluded in that short statement. (This has been a very controversial subject and it is not our goal to cover the scientific topics but to cover spiritual ones.) And then verse two followed, making it even more confusing.

> *"And the earth was without form, and void: and darkness was upon the face of the deep. And the Spirit of God moved upon the face of the waters."*

These two verses leave a lot for our imagination to try and figure out.

Time issues:

- When was the beginning?
- Does our Bible include the history of earth from the original creation?
- If so, how do we reconcile the age of dinosaurs with time of Adam's creation?

Biblical issues:

- Did God create the earth without form, void and dark?
- Would God create an earth made so imperfectly? "His works are perfect and full of glory!" *Deuteronomy. 32:4 and Psalms 111:3*
- Everything that God created in the first chapter of the Bible, God stated was "GOOD" except the earth itself. Why?

The confusion of the first two verses is the result of an incorrect translation of one word in the original Hebrew. The basic meaning in the biblical 'lexicon' for the Hebrew word "was" in verse 2: - a verb meaning "fall out, come to pass, become, be, happen, occur, and came to pass". In other Scriptures in the King James Bible, the same word is translated "and it came to pass or became". The Scripture could have been translated: And the earth BECAME without form, and void. So let's read it, as it is translated in the Message Bible with the word "became"... not was.

> *"First this: God created the Heavens and Earth - all you see, all you don't see. Earth "became" a soup of nothingness, a bottomless emptiness, an inky blackness. God's Spirit brooded like a bird above the watery abyss."*

So what caused it to "become" such a state of confusion? And when did it happen? How long was the earth in that condition when God decided to take another look at his earthly kingdom and decided to revitalize or refurbish it back to it perfect condition?

Scientists say the earth shows proof that it is millions, if not billions of years old. According to their studies, cave men lived on the earth during the Paleolithic Era, sometimes called the Stone Age, which was 10,000 years ago (and could go back to over 2 million years). Dinosaurs also make us question the age of earth. Recently discovered prosauropods dinosaur remains from Madagascar (which are the oldest that have been found) are about 230 million years old.

So how old is the earth and how much time occurred between verse one when God originally created the earth and when it "became" void and full of confusion? Does the Bible give us any help about what happened? And what would have made God so angry that he allowed the earth to become void without form?

In most of the Bible, the Prophets <u>look into the future</u>. But in this particular situation, we need a prophet to <u>look back into time</u>. The Prophet Jeremiah did just that and gave us a hint of what happen.

> *"I looked at the earth – it was back to pre-genesis chaos and emptiness. I looked at the skies, and not a star to be seen. I looked at the mountains – they were trembling like aspen leaves, and all the hills rocking back and forth in the wind. I looked – what's this! Not man or woman in sight, not a bird to be seen in the skies. I looked – this can't be! Every garden and orchard shriveled up. All the towns were ghost towns. And all this because of God, because of the blazing anger of God." Jeremiah 4:23-27*

But what made God so angry that the world shook, the lights went out, all cities were destroyed, and there was no life to be found? Everything that God created as we have already discovered was perfect, so what happened?

When God created the angelic host, he created one who was the most beautiful and most wise of them all, the archangel, Lucifer. He was like a trophy creation and perfect in all his ways. The Prophet Ezekiel was given a vision of him and this is his summation:

> *"You were the anointed cherub. I placed you on the mountain of God. You strolled in magnificence among the stones of fire. From the day of your creation, you were sheer perfection and then imperfection – evil! – was detected in you. In much buying and selling you turned violent, you sinned! I threw you, disgraced, off the mountain of God. I threw you out – you, the*

> *anointed angel-cherub. No more strolling among the gems of fire for you! Your beauty went to your head. You corrupted wisdom by using it to get worldly fame. I threw you to the ground, sent you sprawling before an audience of kings and let them gloat over your demise. By sin after sin after sin, by your corrupt ways of doing business, you defiled your holy places of worship. So I set a fire around and within you. I reduced you to ashes. All anyone sees now when they look for you is ashes, a pitiful mound of ashes. All who once knew you now throw up their hands: This can't have happened! This has happened!" Ezekiel 28:13-19*

When God created this perfect angelic being, he gave Lucifer (also known as Satan) freewill just as he had given all the angels. That freewill allowed him to make choices of good and evil. Until this point, this freewill had always been used to worship and please God. He had used it faithfully; but Satan grew arrogant and decided he was so perfect, he could be God himself. He then sinned and all of heaven and earth felt the results of it.

> *"What a comedown this, O Babylon...! Flat on your face in the underworld mud, you, famous for flattening nations! You said to yourself,*
>
> - *'I'll climb to heaven.*
> - *I'll set my throne over the stars of God.*
> - *I'll run the assembly of angels that meet on sacred Mount Zaphon.*
> - *I'll climb to the top of the clouds.*
> - *I'll take over as King of the Universe!'*
>
> *But you didn't make it, did you? Instead of climbing up, you came down" Isaiah 14:12-15*

Rebellion in the Kingdom of God, against God himself, would cause the anger that Jeremiah had seen in the vision of chaos on the earth. Satan and a number of other heavenly angels chose rebellion against God, causing them to lose all God had originally blessed them with and he threw Satan and his rebellious angels to the earth. Isaiah, the Prophet, indicates that Satan was thrown down to earth and caused some sort of confusion and the Earth became void without form. God did this as a result of his anger at Lucifer! In *Luke 10:18, "Jesus said, I saw Satan fall, a bolt of lightning out of the sky."* The earth at that point was the kingdom of the world being run by Satan. But God still owned the earth and he had a better plan - the earthly land would be redeemed and it would once again become Kingdom of God for his redemptive plan for mankind.

After thousands and thousands of years (no one knows for sure how many), God knew that if he created a new man with freewill that, that very freewill would also cause him to sin. So already knowing this, God created a plan to reconcile man back to himself. Therefore, the destiny of earth and God's kingdom on earth had to be reconstructed! How much time and what happened between verse one and two could fill thousands of books, but in the end, it is not for us to know at this time. Some truths are being held from us until we get to heaven and God will reveal all to us and we will see clearly.

If we continue on in Genesis 1, after the second verse, God put all thing on earth together again to perfection and then he created the first man, Adam, on day 6 of the story of creation.

> *"God spoke. 'Let us make human beings in our own image, make them reflecting our nature. So they can be responsible for the fish in the sea, the birds in the air, the cattle, and, yes, Earth itself, and ever animal that moves on the face of Earth'. God created human beings, he created them godlike, reflecting God's nature. He created them male and female. God created man in his own image, in the image of God created he him; male and female created he them.*
>
> *"God blessed them: 'Prosper! Reproduce! Fill Earth! Take charge! Be responsible for fish in the sea and birds in the air, for everything that moves on the face of Earth!' Then God said, 'I've given you every sort of seed-bearing plant on Earth and every kind of fruit-bearing tree given them to you for food. To all animals and all birds, everything that moves and breathes, I give whatever grows out of the ground for food.' And there it was. God looked over everything he had made; it was so good, so very good! It was evening, it was morning - Day Six." Genesis 1*

The kingdom of earth was once again joined to God and his kingdom! Since then the Bible documents the important events from creation to the end of earth as we know it, as described in the Book of Revelation. During the early days of earth, humanity would do just as God had predicted. Through the temptation of Satan,

Eve was confused by Satan's words and Adam willingly chose his own will over God's will and ate the apple from the Tree of Good and Evil in the Garden of Eden. Until this point, God had provided a perfect place for his human creation but his crafty fallen angel had brought destruction once again to the earth by their will to sin against God's perfect plan. As a result of God's all pre-knowledge of sin, he already had a plan in place to restore humanity into right fellowship with their Creator once again.

The process of complete reconciliation was not a quick plan in the eyes of man but in God's timetable, it could have been said that it took the same number of days to create the earth, animals, vegetation and Adam as it took to reconcile the sin of Adam. The completion cycle will take approximately 6000 years. Let me explain how 6 days to create the earth and man equals 6000 years to complete God's predetermined plan of redeeming the sin that resulted from Adam's freewill. In 1 Peter 3:8, Peter says:

> *"Don't overlook the obvious here, friends. With God, one day is as good as a thousand years, a thousand years as a day."*

The scholars of the Bible have documented that the time that follows the fall of Adam until complete redemption can be divided into four time periods.

1. Creation to destruction with the Flood of Noah's time - 2000 years
2. Flood to the birth of Jesus Christ – 2000 years
3. Jesus birth, life and death to his return to earth leading up to the millennium – 2000 years
4. The Millennium -1000 years

The six days of creation equals the 6000 years from creation to Jesus' last return to earth. The seventh day of rest will be represented as the millennial time - a thousand years of perfect peace on the earth when the earth will be restored to original perfection.

The first 2000 years was man populating the earth and establishing to the best of his ability a kingdom satisfactory for relationship with God. However, Noah was the only human that God was pleased with.

> *"God said: 'I'll get rid of my ruined creation, make a clean sweep: people, animals, snakes and bugs, birds – the works. I'm sorry I made them.' But*

> *Noah was different. God liked what he saw in Noah…Noah was a good man, a man of integrity in his community. Noah walked with God…As far as God was concerned, the Earth had become a sewer; there was violence everywhere. God took one look and saw how bad it was, everyone corrupt and corrupting—life's itself corrupt to the core. God said: 'It's all over. It's the end of the human race'…" Genesis 6:7-13*

However, God made a covenant with Noah and his family based on their lives of integrity to God and his ways. Through their family, man populated the earth again. And during the next 2000 years God provided a way for man to establish a blood relationship through animal sacrifice to cover their sins in order to maintain fellowship with a sinless God.

God's purpose during this time was for man to grow in understanding of God's ways. And with Noah's family bloodline of faithfulness to God, the Jewish nation would be established. The Jews would be his chosen people and their human bloodline, through Mary, would unite with God's bloodline to birth the second God-head, Jesus. This was accomplished through Mary, being a virgin mother, allowing the Holy Spirit (the third God-head) to supernaturally impregnate her, and the blood of God would be passed to human man.

Jesus', our Savior, mission was to bring the Kingdom of God to the earth. He was commissioned in heaven to accomplish this by God the Father, himself. After Jesus' birth, the Kingdom of God would be preached during this last 2000 years.

It was John the Baptist who introduced the idea of kingdom during his personal ministry, paving the way for Jesus. His cry in the wilderness announced that we had changes on the horizon.

> *"While Jesus was living in the Galilean Hills, John, called 'the Baptizer', was preaching in the desert country of Judea. His message was simple and austere, like his desert surroundings: 'Change your life. God's Kingdom is here'." Matthew 3:1-2*

What did John the Baptist mean when he said: God's kingdom is here? John knew he was the pre-runner for someone better than himself, God's great redeemer, Jesus. John was aware and watching for Jesus' appearance to introduce him and his mission to the Jewish nation. The people were pouring out to see John the

Baptist and he was well-known as a plain man of the wilderness who was proclaiming that he was doing a baptism of repentance (it was not a baptism of salvation). It is certain that John was not contradicting what had been spiritual truths for generations as far back as Abraham. But he was teaching that things where changing and the old ways of the Pharisees (religious priests) and their religious acts, would be done away with. He was letting Jewish people know they needed to prepare for a new spirituality, where each person would have to meet the requirements of the new kingdom and be responsible for their own God-given destiny. John the Baptist explained that Jesus, the new baptizer would...

> *"turn their old life in for a kingdom life. The real action would come next. The main character in this drama--compared to him, who would be a mere stagehand--will ignite the kingdom life within them, a fire within them, the Holy Spirit within them, changing them from the inside out. He's going to clean house--make a clean sweep of their lives. He'll place everything true in it proper place before God; everything false he'll put out with the trash to be burned." Matthew 3:11-12*

And then, Jesus appeared one day to be baptized while John was in the Jordan River baptizing new believers. As Jesus came up out of the water, the skies opened up and the Spirit of God in the form of a dove, descended on him and a voice from heaven introduced Jesus,

> *"This is my Son, chosen and marked by my love, delight of my life." Matthew 3:17*

John's baptism was a preview of the baptism that Jesus would introduce. John's was for repentance, while Jesus' was for salvation of those who accepted him as the Son of God and their redeemer. John's baptism was a beginning step in the right direction for the men of the old covenant and the new baptism was for the "new kingdom man". As a result, John got to baptize Jesus as the first man under the new covenant.

Jesus was the first new covenant man, born on earth. His earthly mother was Mary, a virgin. She was overcome by the Holy Spirit (part of the God-Head - the three in one - God the Father, God the Son and the Holy Spirit) who impregnated her with "God's Blood". No human man was involved. Therefore, Jesus was the first man that could be called born-again and qualified for the baptism of water. When John baptized Jesus, a dove descended out of heaven. This also represented the Holy Spirit's approval and was a preview of his presentation in the kingdom after Jesus' death.

This dove was sent from God with two purposes:

- A message to all, that Jesus was his son in whom he was well pleased.
- To anoint Jesus with the Holy Spirit for performing his destiny.

It was at this time that Jesus was given the power and authority of God to introduce and live kingdom life on earth in the "New Kingdom of Heaven/God".

This same anointing and authority would later be given to the disciples and all born-again believers after Jesus' death and resurrection. It was Jesus' legal right to receive it as a result of being born of woman with the blood of God running through his earthly body. God, himself, gave Jesus that Holy Ghost authority and after his resurrection, Jesus told the disciples that they should go to Jerusalem and wait to receive the baptism of the Holy Spirit with power!

After Jesus' baptism by John the Baptist, he was tested in the wilderness. Three times Satan would tempt Jesus, trying to get him out of the will of God...to sin! Each time, Jesus quoted Scriptures from the Old Testament to show his authority to Satan. The last temptation was Satan offering Jesus his kingdoms of the earth with all of its glory but Jesus already possessed authority over the earth as a part of the God-Head. Satan would only possess temporary authority until Jesus would die and go to Hell to take the "Keys" from Satan. His response was simple and direct:

> *"Worship the Lord your God and only him. Serve him with absolute single-heartedness." Matthew 3:10.*

From that moment forward, Jesus would be teaching and preaching the concept of the Kingdom of God (interchanged with the title Kingdom of Heaven).

Jesus' primary reason for coming to earth was to destroy Satan and his work on the earth. This was God's original plan that was developed at the fall of Lucifer, and would be executed in order to reconcile humanity to himself when Adam choose his will over God's will.

And how would Jesus destroy Satan's destructive powers? 1 Peter 5:8 tells us that our adversary the devil, acts as a roaring lion, walking about seeking whom he may devour. He lies, steals and destroys everything in his path that is of God, but Jesus overcame the evil of Satan and his demons. Jesus overcame it all: poverty, sickness and spiritual death of man by healing, delivering and working miracles AND teaching the principles of kingdom life to his new followers.

Kingdom Thinking

At what age did you accept Christ? What was the situation around it? Were you in a crisis? What were some of the immediate changes in your new Born-again experience?

After accepting life in the Kingdom of God, how did your changing residency to the new kingdom change your daily life? Was the change immediate? If not how would you describe the change?

After reviewing the chart, did you see more clearly the difference between the two kingdoms? Do you feel that non-Christians would have an easier time accepting Jesus if they understood the Contrast? Why?

The list of differences between the Kingdom of God and the kingdom of Satan are many. See if you can come up with four additional contrasts. Star any that you saw in your life?

Did the first two verses in the Bible ever confuse you? Clarifying the translation of "was" to "became as" really helped me understand the creation of earth. Did the consequences of rebellion help you clarify the earth being without form and void?

Explain how God's blood was transferred into Jesus' Bloodline.

Keys to the Kingdom

- There is a definite difference between the Kingdom of God and the kingdom of Satan
- Quality of your life depends on which kingdom you reside in.
- God had a plan for planet earth from the beginning of time.
- Rebellion causes chaos and death.
- The earth has dual kingdoms on it.
- The bloodline of God resides in Jesus.
- The Kingdom of God was introduced by Jesus and his ministry.
- Jesus came to destroy the evil of Satan and his kingdom.

CHAPTER 3

Kingdom Culture

Promises and Transfer of Authority

It was a typical hot Texas summer and no relief could be found on the evening weather report. Yet everyone in the family was weary and needing a break from the heat. The temperatures were predicted to be breaking 100 degrees the next week and you can be sure that in Houston's cement jungle, it would feel 10-15 degrees hotter than the reports.

I had purchased a 3 day – 2 night mini-vacation at a charity auction the previous year and decided maybe it was the right time to gather up my son's family and head to the hill country to cool off. Just a 4 hour drive away is a wonderful German community known for the Comal River that runs through the center of town. The river is fed by icy-cold springs-water from the Edward's Plateau aquifer and the water temperature stays around 65-75 degrees all year. The town is a wonderful get-away and just what was needed to break the Texas heat on the coastal plains near Galveston Bay. Two days to just lay back in a tube and float down the river with no worries, no concerns and relax. And that is just what the family needed.

On the second evening after our cool float down the river, we decided to go exploring in the hill country for a quaint place to have dinner. We ended up in a small serene town called Wimberley. The main drag, through the heart of the town, was lined with beautiful old-fashioned country stores filled with arts and crafts and places to eat. After a traditional Texas country fried steak dinner, we traveled down a windy country road where we found a pioneer western town that had been built as a movie set for a Hallmark movie filmed earlier that spring. My six year old granddaughter had requested ice cream for dessert after dinner and guess what the old town had opened for tourists that explored it? An Old Fashion Ice Cream Parlor! Life just doesn't get much better after a wonderful day like we had, unless it has some Texas Bluebell ice cream to finish it off. As I drove us back to our cottage on the river, we travelled through the hills; we watched the sun go down with a spectacular Texas sunset. We were thanking God for our wonderful day, when in a split second of time, the last sun rays bursting with color hit the windshield and blinded me! A deer jumped out from behind a bush along the road, in direct line to hit the front bumper of the car. It was so close, I could see the deer's eyelashes. In that same moment, I screamed…. "STOP in Jesus name!" I am not sure how it all happened. But we were saved from a horrible accident. Whether an angel stood between the car and the deer or if an invisible wall broke the deer's leap, I don't know but somehow the deer did not hit us and all I could see in the rear view mirror was the deer standing in the road, unhurt.

I had prayed for safety as I always do before the trip. I had complete faith in my prayers being answered, but little did I know, that Satan would challenge my faith and my authority by attempting to take all of our lives that evening. In the beginning when God created the earth, man and the animals, God gave man authority over animals. That authority would be tested in that quick moment in time. God saved us by performing a miracle. He honored his Word and utilized the transfer of authority to me, his believer, which he promised!

Let's look at how much God loves us and why we were saved.

God's Original Authority

God's reason for making man in his own image was for companionship. He desired someone to have relationship with. He also wanted to share his glory and his authority.

God spoke on the 6th day:

> *"Let US make HUMAN BEINGS in OUR image, make them reflecting OUR nature so they can be RESPONSIBLE for the fish in the sea, the birds in the air, the cattle, and yes, Earth itself, and every animal that moves on the face of Earth." Genesis 1:26* (Caps for significance)

As I read this Scripture, it is AS IF, God the Father, God the Son and the Holy Spirit were in an important business meeting. As the Corporate Officers of the universe, they are sharing the outcome of their creation (a new corporate business adventure) called earth. They sat around the corporate conference table and looked at all that resulted in the development phase:

1. They (the three of them) looked at the confusion and void and the Spirit moved upon the watery abyss and God said "LET THERE BE LIGHT" and it appeared.
2. Then God separated the light from darkness
3. God spoke: "Sky! In the middle of the waters, SEPARATE water from water." Therefore, His words separated the water in the clouds from the water in the sea.
4. God spoke: "SEPARATE! Water-beneath-Heaven, gather into one place: Land, APPEAR!"
5. God spoke: "Earth, GREEN UP! Grow all varieties of seed-bearing plants, every sort of fruit-bearing tree."
6. God spoke: "Lights! COME OUT! Shine in Heaven's sky! SEPARATE! Day and Night." The heavenly objects gave help for the earth's inhabitance to trace the seasons, and days and years. The lights in the heavens were the Sun, Moon and stars.
7. God spoke: "SWARM, oceans, with fish and sea life! Birds, fly through the sky over earth." The skies and the waters were filled with creatures. God blessed them by speaking: "PROSPER! REPRODUCE!"
8. God spoke: "Earth, GENERATE life! And all kinds of reptiles, insects and animals, both domestic and wild, appeared on the land."
   (Based on Genesis Chapter 1)

After the Corporate Officers reviewed all they had made, they realized they needed someone to manage it all! It was quite a creation! Just as they had created Lucifer to oversee the angels, they decided they would make "man" to oversee the earth. The Bible doesn't give us all the details of what man would be like but it does say, he would be made in Gods image and be a reflection of the God-Head's nature. *"Let us make human beings in OUR image, make them reflecting OUR nature so they could be responsible for... handling and managing creation"* Genesis 1:26. Only the Officers (God-Head) would know; but they gave MAN everything he would need. The God-Head had authority over the earth and all of His creatures and they gave that authority to the man that they had created.

Man was entirely different from all the rest of God's diverse creatures. The man God made had:

- A soul (mind) that could reason and think like God the Father.
- A body that had a physical presence on earth like Jesus.
- A spirit which could communicate and praise God like the Holy Spirit.

This man God created was made to be spiritually in tune with the Tri-head God and His creations.

In any corporation, the management team is very important for the success of the company. However, there are times when members of the team make wrong decisions causing the whole corporate team to pay for the mistake. These wrong decisions are usually made when the manager is not in tune spiritually with the corporate officers. When this happens in God's kingdom, these mistakes are called sins.

Satan sinned when he made the decision that he wanted to replace the God of the universe. The result was God cast him out of heaven. Satan made the first wrong decision and now it was Satan himself coming into God's garden to cause confusion in the new kingdom by making man an offer that would lead Adam to eat the fruit of the Tree of Knowledge of Good and Evil. Everything, changed when Adam and Eve decided to eat the fruit from the forbidden tree. Now man had sinned also.

It may seem that the encounter with Satan happened shortly after God had created Adam and Eve; however, that is only opinion. Many scholars say that no one knows how long they got to enjoy the benefits God intended for them in the garden. I believe God's home for them enthralled them with its beauty and its ability to meet every need they had. The timing of Satan's appearance was very important for his success to turn their satisfaction of God's provision into enough dissatisfaction to entertain the idea of disobeying God's direct command not to eat the fruit. What and when this happened is not known. What is known is when they committed the first sin, they lost protection and provision in the garden and they were cast out into the unprotected areas of the earth. One of the greatest things they lost that God had intended for them to have, was their authority over everything in God's kingdom.

Four thousand years later when Jesus died on the cross, everything that Adam and Eve lost in the garden, was restored to their spiritual descendants, who accepted God's new conditions for mankind to return to right standing with him. This would once again open the door to the benefits of the kingdom life. As a result of Jesus' crucifixion, death and resurrection, we can now walk in righteousness. This allows us to conquer the earthly domain that Satan stole and therefore, advance God's kingdom again.

To understand what we have re-gained, we must first define the "Kingdom of God" on earth. During Jesus' ministry on earth, he taught kingdom principles many times. Let's explore what is recorded in the Bible. Jesus explained to the Roman authorities that God's kingdom was a spiritual reality.

> *"My kingdom doesn't consist of what you see around you. If it did, my followers would fight so that I wouldn't be handed over to the Jews. But I'm not that kind of king, not the world's kind of king...Because I am king, I was born and entered the world so that I could witness to the truth. Everyone who cares for truth, who has any feeling for the truth, recognizes my voice." John 18:36-37*

Jesus also explained the Kingdom of God to his disciples this way:

> *"The kingdom of God doesn't come by counting the days on the calendar. Nor when someone says, 'Look here!' or, 'There it is!' And why? Because God's kingdom is already among you."* or the King James Bible explains it this way, *"Kingdom of God is within you." Luke 17:20-21*

Nicodemus, one of the Pharisees of Jesus' time, was confused, when Jesus personally explained the Kingdom of God to him. Let's visit Jesus' conversation with him. Nicodemus stated,

> *"Rabbi, we all know you're a teacher straight from God. No one could do all the God-pointing, God-revealing acts you do if God weren't in on it. Jesus said, 'You're absolutely right. Take it from me: Unless a person is born from above, it's not possible to see what I'm pointing to—God's Kingdom.'*
>
> Nicodemus asked, *"How can anyone be born who has already been born and grown up? You can't re-enter your mother's womb and be born again. What are you saying with 'born from above' talk?"*

"Jesus said, "You're not listening. Let me say it again. Unless a person submits to this original creation—the wind hovering over the water creation, the invisible moving the visible, a baptism into a new life—it is not possible to enter God's Kingdom. When you look at a baby, it's just that: a body you can look at and touch. But the person who takes shape within is formed by something you can't see and touch—the Spirit—and becomes a living spirit. So don't be so surprised when I tell you that you have to be 'born from above'—out of this world, so to speak. You know well enough how the wind blows this way and that. You hear it rustling through the trees, but you have no idea where it comes from or where it's headed next. That's the way it is with everyone 'born from above' by the wind of God, the spirit of God."

Nicodemus asked, *"What do you mean by this? How does this happen? Jesus said, 'You're a respected teacher of Israel and you don't know these basics? Listen carefully. I'm speaking sober truth to you. I speak only of what I know by experience; I give witness only to what I have seen with my own eyes. There is nothing secondhand here, no hearsay. Yet instead of facing the evidence and accepting it, you procrastinate with questions. If I tell you things that are plain as the hand before your face and you don't believe me, what use is there in telling you things you can't see, the things of God? No one has ever gone up into the presence of God except the One who came down from that Presence, the Son of Man. In the same way that Moses lifted the serpent in the desert so people could have something to see and then believe, it is necessary for the Son of Man to be lifted up—and everyone who looks up to him, trusting and expectant, will gain a real life, eternal life. This is how much God loved the world; He gave his Son, his one and only Son. And this is why: so that no one need to be destroyed; by believing in him, anyone can have a whole and lasting life. God didn't go to all the trouble of sending his Son merely to point an accusing finger, telling the world how bad it was. He came to help put the world right again. Anyone who trusts in him is acquitted; anyone who refuses to trust him has long since been under the death sentence without knowing it. And why? Because of that person's failure to believe in the one-of-a-kind Son of God when introduced to him.'*

'This is the crisis we're in: God-light streamed into the world, but men and women everywhere ran for the darkness. They went for the darkness because they were not really interested in pleasing God. Everyone who makes a practice of doing evil, addicted to denial and illusion, hates God-light and won't come near it, fearing a painful exposure. But anyone working and living in truth and reality welcomes God-light so the work can be seen for the God-work it is'." John 3:2-21

Nicodemus was so hungry for the truth of "Kingdom Life" and Kingdom of God, that while he was with Jesus, he wanted to make sure that Jesus clarified the process of receiving all God had for him. Jesus explained, in great detail, the transformation of accepting Jesus, himself, as the Son of God.

If you are reading this and have any doubt that you have been born again, now is the time to make sure! If you don't have the fruit of salvation in your life or don't see a change in your life, it is time you stop and pray a simple faith prayer! Nicodemus was a priest but he questioned Jesus to make sure he understood. Many say they are "Christians" but they do not understand that just attending church does not make you "Born Again"! Let's re-visit this conversation and list the things Jesus said. Then decide what your real standing with God is:

- A person needs to be submitted to God the Creator
- A person must be born from above, by the Spirit of God
- A person must accept that God sent Jesus to earth, born of a virgin and fathered by the Spirit of God, himself
- A person must believe that Jesus, God's only Son, died on the cross for their sins
- A person must trust in Jesus when they are introduced to him
- A person must be willing to walk in God's truth and let God lead them into the Kingdom of God
- A person must accept these things and have faith that they are true. YOU must accept these things and say a simple prayer of faith!

A Prayer of Faith for Salvation

Jesus, I come to you today to ask you to be Lord of my life.

I ask you to forgive me for my sins and restore me to right standing with you.

I confess that you came to earth for this purpose,

That you were born of a virgin and you are God in human flesh.

While you were here on earth, you showed me how to live my life.

And then gave your life for me.

You died on the cross, were buried and raised back to life after 3 days.

Now you sit in heaven at the right hand of God the Father to intercede for me.

Thank you for giving me a new life and leading me into your kingdom.

Guide me in your ways. Fill me with your Spirit so that I can be the person you have called me to be. Help me find my destiny.

In Jesus' name, Amen

It is the easiest crossing over in your life to cross over from death to eternal life—by accepting Jesus. A simple prayer can do more than trying to work your way into the kingdom of God by being good and doing good things. It is a confession of faith. However, as simple as that sounds, for some people, to be able to exercise their faith without having a complete understanding of every detail, is not easy. The Bible says over and over that *"without faith it is impossible to please God!" Hebrews 11:6 KJ* Impossible!

Paul the Apostle was a great example of this. His name before he was saved was Saul of Tarsus. He hated the Christians of the early church and as a Roman, he persecuted Christians as often as possible. He would go *"wild, devastating the church, entering house after house after house, dragging men and women off to jail." Acts 8:3.* He, more than any other man of Jesus time, tried to stop the kingdom movement from happening. He had no faith or belief that Jesus was sent from God to save the world. All he personally wanted to do was hurt men and women who believed differently than he did.

How do you think God handled such a man? God wants everyone to make up their own mind if they will choose to follow Jesus. How did God change Saul of Tarsus, a man who persecuted Christians, into Paul, an apostle of Jesus, who dedicated the rest of his life to converting everyone to Jesus as their Savior? God did it...with LOVE, MERCY and GRACE! Saul wanted to destroy Christianity but God showed him these attributes and instead, Saul/Paul became a world-changing Christian and one of the greatest soul winners in history. In his later years, he wrote more of the New Testament than any other man. Here is his story.

Saul was on the road to Damascus with arrest warrants which allowed him to arrest any man or woman who belonged to the Christian Church and take them to Jerusalem for persecution.

> *"When he got to the outskirts of Damascus, he was suddenly dazed by a blinding flash of light. As he fell to the ground, he heard a voice: 'Saul, Saul, why are you out to get me? '*He *said, 'Who are you, Master?' 'I am Jesus, the One you're hunting down. I want you to get up and enter the city.' In the city you'll be told what to do next." Acts 9:3-6*

Saul's life was about to be changed forever. He was on a mission to kill and destroy but God had a better and more meaningful purpose for him. In that moment, God touch him with his MERCY. For a period of time, God allowed Saul to lose his physical sight, in order for his spiritual eyes to be opened. Saul didn't desire God's mercy, but God gave it to him so he could see the things of God. While he was blinded by light from heaven, Saul had a vision from God that gave him directions to go to Damascus where a man named Ananias would restore his sight. The Roman soldiers that were with Saul to help accomplish his original mission continued in obedience to Saul and led blind Saul on to Damascus. For three days, Saul prayed and waited for God's disciple, Ananias. God also directed Ananias by the Holy Spirit to go to the street called "Straight" and tell Saul, he was the man in Saul's vision who would place his hands on Saul's eyes for healing. When Ananias got to the house, Saul had already had an encounter with the God of the universe and given his life over to him. Ananias knew that Saul was already saved and called Saul his Christian brother, even though he knew Saul had been a hater of the Christians for years. Ananias knew if the Holy Spirit sent him to lay hands on Saul, then his life had been touched by Jesus. Ananias laid his hands on Saul's eyes and his eyes were healed and he could see again. Saul's life had been radically touched by Jesus' mercy.

Saul was also touched by his GRACE. He certainly had not deserved to be healed, saved or filled with the Holy Spirit. But because of Paul's faith, he took action and prayed and God heard him and saved Paul by his grace. We are all saved the same way. We don't deserve salvation, the forgiveness of our sins or the benefits of the Kingdom of God on our own merits, but God so loved the world that he expresses it to each of us with his LOVE that only he can give.

God changed his name from Saul to Paul, the Apostle, and gave him a whole new identity. Old things had passed away and a new man, with a new spirit and a new destiny was left in his place. His story brings clarity to what happens when we decide to follow Jesus; we change our home from the kingdom of earth to the Kingdom of God and our purposes change to God's purpose for us. Paul said it this way in 1 Corinthians:

> *"We follow this sequence in Scripture: The First Adam received life, the Last Adam (JESUS) is a life-giving Spirit. Physical life comes first, then spiritual—a firm base shaped from the earth, a final completion coming out of heaven. The First Man was made out of earth, and people since then are earthly; the Second Man was made out of heaven, and people now can be heavenly. In the same way that we've worked from earthly origins, let's embrace our heavenly ends. I need to emphasize friends that our natural, earthly lives don't in themselves lead us by their very nature into the kingdom of God. Their very "nature is to die, so how could they "naturally" end up in the life kingdom?*
>
> *But let me tell you something wonderful, a mystery I'll probably never fully understand. We're not all going to die—but we are all going to be changed." 1 Corinthians 15:45-52*

After our experience of meeting God's mercy, grace and love, we are all going to change from one glory to the next glory until we are as fine gold that is refined to the point that God can see his own image in our face.

Jesus' kingdom is a spiritual dominion that is constantly increasing within our hearts and lives, causing us to change our own sphere of life and all of creation around us. It is a spiritual force that starts in our heart and is manifested in righteousness, derived by faith and expressed through love.

By choosing to follow Jesus, we are made righteousness. Jesus died that we might be his righteousness on earth. This is not something we can do out of our own strength but it can only be obtained through faith in Christ. This kind of righteousness helps us to do the right thing; such as, love others as Jesus has loved us.

Many years ago, I sponsored three Mexican young men for instruction in a Bible School in Torrean, Mexico. When they graduated they came for a visit to see me in Houston, Texas. It was a special time that God gave me, to show his love for my obedience. They brought me a gift as a Thank-you for my support in their spiritual life. It was a gold necklace with my name, "JOY" engraved inside of a heart. Around the edge of the necklace were the words, Jesus, Others and You. They said I had shown them Jesus' love for them by setting an example that this necklace represented. I had put Jesus first in my life, had given myself to others (them), and put myself last in order to help them know God's love for them. They couldn't have given me anything that would have pleased me more. I wear the necklace proudly and remember my goal: to let others see Jesus in my life. Thank you guys, I hope you are living those goals in your life.

The necklace shows God's kind of righteousness and not any self-righteousness of our own making. It is the righteousness of God that gives us the dominion in his kingdom. In Psalms 45:6-7, it quotes one of my favorite Scriptures:

"Your throne is God's Throne, ever and always;

The scepter of your royal rule measures right living.

You love the right and hate the wrong.

And that is why God, your very own God,

Poured fragrant oil on your head,

Making you out as king from among your dear companions."

A scepter is a very ornate rod that serves as a symbol of power and authority in the hands of a ruler. It represents the king's authority and dominion, just as a signet ring represents the king's seal of approval for the message inside the enclosure. This Scripture's scepter is decorated with righteousness which is his authority. It is an extension of his rule measured by the extension of his righteousness. Another way of describing it is - the Kingdom of God is the kingdom of "Righteousness, Peace and Joy, in the Holy Spirit".

It is our purpose to be that extension of God's dominion and rule over the earth. God is at the center of everything. All revolves around him and he has the last word about everything. God wants to restore to his church the dominion and power that Satan took with the fall of man. God gave the authority over to Jesus and he has authority over the church. The church is Christ's body, under Jesus' dominion and he uses us (the church) to speak, act and fill everything with his presence. (Ephesians 1:22-23)

When I started public school at 6 years old, I also started my training to become a priest and king. In my immature state as a child, I did not understand the purpose of this training. Let me explain. It was a curriculum in the Baptist church called GA's. Its purpose was to train us in spirit, words and action to be an outstanding member in God's church. One of our primary activities was to memorize the Word of God. It started out in first grade with becoming a "maiden" and learning simple Scriptures like "Arise, shine for the light has come". And after 12 years of studying God's Word and using it in actions of service for the church, you become a "Queen with a Scepter" by memorizing, "The Sermon on the Mount" as a senior in High School. In between, were "Maid in Waiting", "Princess", "Queens", etc. As I progressed through the program, I grew in knowledge, wisdom and authority in the Kingdom of God. I didn't realize then what I was doing, which was preparing myself to become royalty in God's kingdom. It would affect me throughout my lifetime. The scepter given to me represented the groundwork which has guided me into the authority and power of Christ that I walk in today. Through it, I was prepared for my earthly title with responsibilities of king and priest for my God.

We are meant to be an extension of Jesus' righteous rule:

> *"...Slain! Paying in blood, you bought men and women, brought them back from all over the earth, Bought them back for God. Then you made them a Kingdom, Priest for our God, Priest-king to rule over the earth." Revelation 5:9-10*

Through Jesus' righteousness, we have the same dominion and authority on the earth as a priestly king. How do we display that dominion and authority? Only by being a reflection of him. Our display of his authority is dependent on our obedience and our preparation in the spiritual realm.

It is our inheritance! God gladly transfers his authority over to us, so we can do the works of Jesus. The Word of God says we can rule and reign on the earth!

We not only inherit the title and authority but we also inherit the tools to get the job done. Let's take a look at some of the things God says about us.

- We are chosen for the high calling of priestly work, chosen to be a holy people, God's instruments to do his work and speak out for him, to tell others of the night-and-day difference he made, taking us from nothing to something, from rejected to accepted. 1 Peter 2:9-10
- We are in Christ. God put the wrong on Jesus, who never did anything wrong, so we could be put right with him. 2 Corinthians 5:21
- We are more than conquerors in Christ. Romans 8:37
- We are partakers of the inheritance of the saints Colossians 1:12
- We live in the Kingdom of God and are fellow citizens with the saints of the household of God. Ephesians 2:19
- We are the light of the world and the salt of the earth to express God to others. Matthew 5:13-14
- We are the hope of glory with Christ in us. Colossians 1:27
- We have the mind of Christ. Philippians 2:5
- We have overcome the world by our faith in God. 1 John 5:4
- We were predestined to do God's will and receive his inheritance. Ephesians 1:11
- We have received power, power to heal the sick, power to cast out demons, power over our enemy and nothing shall harm us. Mark 16:17, Luke 17:19
- We can do all things through Christ who strengths us. Philippians 4:13
- We have the greatest one in us to overcome the world; the Holy Spirit! 1 John 4:4

We can always triumph because of all that God gave us when we accepted Jesus, but we must choose to walk in it.

Which is better: power or authority? Both are needed for success in the kingdom. With God's authority through Jesus, you have the power to enforce the authority. Let's take a policeman as an example. He could be small in stature but with his authority he can put a large, powerful man in jail. The badge he wears gives him the authority to do whatever is necessary to control the man. The policeman can blow a small whistle and cars stop to his authority. We are the same. When we declare God's Word or use the name of Jesus, demons hear, fear and respect that authority. We have the same power as Jesus had on earth. Jesus taught his disciples that the authority he transferred to them had that same power.

- *"See what I've given you? Safe passage as you walk on snakes and scorpions, and protection from every assault of the enemy. No one can put a hand on you." Luke 10:19*
- *Jesus gave his charge. "God authorized and commanded me to commission you: Go out and train everyone you meet, far and near, in this life, marking them by baptism in the threefold name: Father, Son, and Holy Spirit. Then instruct them in the practice of all I have commanded you. I'll be with you as you do this, day after day after day, right to the end of the age." Matthew 28:18-20*
- *"What I'm trying to do here is get you to relax, not be so preoccupied with getting so you can respond to God's giving. People who don't know God and the way he works fuss over these things, but you know both God and how he works. Steep yourself in God-reality, God-initiative, God-provision. You'll find all your everyday human concerns will be met. Don't be afraid of missing out... The Father wants to give you the very KINGDOM itself." Luke 12:29-30*

If we want all God has given us, we must be desperate for more of Jesus in our lives. We must seek him with all of our heart! Are you that hungry?

If you are wanting all God has for you, just so you can impress others, you will not get it. If you want to make it difficult and hard, you will miss the simple truth of who Jesus is and what he did for us. You may think you are too inadequate for all this, but God will make sure you get his result regardless, if you seek him. God's Spirit and God's power did it all for us. By activating your faith, God's power and authority is passed on to you. This is wisdom that can't be bought. It is God's wisdom that goes deep into our spirits, for his purposes to bring the best out of us. It is kingdom culture and kingdom wisdom that is passed on to us, his priests and kings, when we are hungry for more of him!

Jesus will always be there for us. He is the charter member of the new covenant and will act as our mediator for all new covenant kings and priests. Jesus sits on a throne in heaven at the right hand of the Father. *"He is in charge of it all, has the final word on everything. At the center of this, Christ rules the church. The church, you see, is not peripheral to the world, the world is peripheral to the church. The church is Christ's body, in which he speaks and acts, by which he fills everything with his presence." Ephesians 1:22-23* If we will do our part, Jesus will do his part to give us the authority and power to overcome the world (Satan) to the end of our days.

Kingdom Thinking:

"Let US make HUMAN BEINGS in OUR image." What does God mean when he said "OUR" image?

God made man in three parts. Explain what they are?

1.

2.

3.

Man was to oversee the Kingdom of God when he was created! When he sinned, what happen to man's authority in the kingdom?

What must man do to be restored to the Kingdom of God?

Define the Kingdom of God on earth that Jesus taught would come after his death?

How did Jesus' death affect the kingdom?

Explain the three God attributes that he uses to save the souls of man.

LOVE

MERCY

GRACE

What is your definition of “Authority” and “Power” in God’s kingdom?

Give 5 examples of restored authority that was regained after Jesus’ resurrection?

List how God describes us as “In Christ”?

Keys to the Kingdom:

- God made man in the image of God the Father, Son and Holy Spirit with:
    1. A soul (mind) that could reason and think like God the Father.
    2. A body that had a physical presence on earth like Jesus.
    3. A spirit which could communicate and praise God like the Holy Spirit.
- God's kingdom is not a physical place but it is spiritual kingdom that is housed in our spirit made possible by Jesus' death and resurrection almost 4000 years after the original sin in the garden.
- Accepting God's provision of salvation and being "Born Again" is an act of faith.
- We do not desire salvation but God wants to give it to us. So, God saved us by LOVE, MERCY and GRACE!
- The Kingdom of God is a spiritual force that starts in our heart and is manifested in righteousness, derived by faith and expressed through love.
- Through Jesus' righteousness, we have the same dominion and authority on the earth as a priestly king. It is our inheritance! God gladly transfers his authority over to us, so we can do the works of Jesus.
- Jesus sits on a throne in heaven at the right hand of the Father. He is in charge of it all, and has the final word on everything. At the center of this, Christ rules the church.

Soaring through Life

by Joy E. Miller

"Soaring Through Life" was painted to remind us that no matter what life may bring your way, you have someone bigger than yourself that will help you!

Do you know that God, the Lord, Creator of Heaven and Earth says...Fainteth not, neither be weary. He will give power to the faint and to those that have no might, he will increase their strength. Even the young shall faint and be weary, but "those who wait on the Lord shall renew their strength...they shall mount up on wings as eagles; they shall run, and not be weary and they shall walk and not faint." *Based on Isaiah 41:28-31*

CHAPTER 4

Kingdom Warfare

Renewing of the Mind

I entered a new year in a deep, dark 'cavern'. It was the blackest and most suffocating place that I had ever experienced. It was devoid of everything I had known. There seemed to be nothing of importance there. It was VOID of all I had experienced and all of my memories. As if everything was erased and I was starting over with only limited remembrance of my previous life. Void of God and his light. Without the light he provided, I could not even describe how bleak and dark it was. It was a place without hope.

Without God's light in our lives there is no knowledge, no wisdom, no hope and therefore, no faith for anything good. Nothing that I had ever learned spiritually was available to me to activate or to help me to overcome the darkness of this place. Oh yes, it actually was available but I couldn't even remember how to reach out to the God of the Universe, who could walk me through the abyss and show me his way out of this cavern of my enemy, my own mind!

Satan was lying to me and I seemed to be buying into his lies. How dark can it get when God's light is not expelling the darkness? Darker than any black I had ever used in painting a picture. No hope to ever get out of the cavern could I find. Satan's lies were trying to take me out. He was trying to stop me from being effective or any kind of asset to the Kingdom of God.

It was as if I was dead spiritually. I kept going to church, doing my Bible studies and all the normal spiritual activities that I had always done. I read God's Word, prayed endlessly, listened to spiritual music and tried to remain in a self-induced spiritual state, but it didn't seem to help. I was a spiritual zombie and nothing was allowing me to walk free of this bondage; to escape this dark place in my mind. Was it a chemical depression or was it a battleground? I cried out in the darkness and yet, I was still defeated. All my formulas for success that I had used before seemed to make no difference. I read my positive confession each morning and turned on worship music at night to calm the darkness. Why could I not see through this darkness? Where was I? Where was God? Why was I in such a defeated place?

I was saying the right things and doing daily life as I had been taught. I desired to be in God's presence and be used by him, but the harder I worked at it, the darker and bleaker it seemed to grow around me. All the religious activities that I had depended on to get me to a successful spiritual level were not working. Why? Was all my work not enough? Was all my knowledge and wisdom I thought I had obtained not enough? Was Satan smarter and more cunning than me? Had he taken me over and I was a sinking ship? Was Satan going to win?

Oh, the battle was terrific and I felt maybe my life was just full of spiritual activity and not spiritual maturity. How could I have fallen for Satan's lies? How did I let the "joy" of the Lord disappear from my daily life?

Sometimes, God lets us experience the darkness so we can see the light. Is this what Job experienced? That is it! It must be a TEST! I so wanted to pass the test...but I seem to be failing it. NO! I screamed. I will not fail!

There were days when I thought I had rounded the corner and could see a break in the darkness. A glimmer of hope, a ray of light, but I wasn't ready to take the right steps to follow up. What was the next step? I heard in my spirit: OBEDIENCE! Obedience to do what God was telling me to do. You see I had sacrificially done the religious things, done the 1, 2, 3's steps, but God was wanting more of me. He wasn't just looking for me to be a happy and prosperous Christian so the world could say how blessed I was because I was following Jesus. Oh, He wants that too, but he wanted more from me. He wanted me to go to new levels with him and I was comfortable with the status quo.

He was trying to take my hand and lead me to a deeper walk with him and yet I wasn't wanting to do it his way. I wanted to do it my way. This was an old pattern for me. I had asked him to take me deeper in my walk with him. I had desired to run through the valleys with him, to experience his love as it is described in Song of Solomon. I want to be prepared as his Bride for his coming return to earth, when he would set up his kingdom of heaven on earth. I wanted to be ready and have my lamp full of oil and burning for others to see; but I didn't want to leave my place of comfort for it. I wanted it to be a personal walk with just the two of us, but he wanted more from me. What did he want?

OBEDIENCE OVER SACRIFICE

God was calling me to new levels of obedience. I thought I had proven myself and my loyalty to him by my works. To go deeper, I could not continue to sacrifice through my works but I would be required to grow and learn new ways...new kingdom ways for the next level!

I had wasted 5 months sacrificing in the cavern, in the darkness, without the light in order to do it my way. I was sacrificing and living with the techniques of the last season. He was answering my prayers to go to the next level but it must be done his way, not mine. Once again the question he presented me with...

Will I do my will or will I do God's will?

Jesus faced this question the night before he was crucified. He wanted to do God's will. He had sacrificed a lot over his thirty years of service and he had always been obedient to do God's will. He had lived a perfect life. He had lived God's principles for others to see and to show it was possible. And he wanted to do God's will but this was his greatest challenge and he must pass the test to accomplish all God planned for man's redemption. To die on the cross and take the weight of humanity's sin on himself, would mean separation from God for a short time and he did not want to face that time alone. He did not want to take the punishment, the physical beating, the ridicule and death that he knew would be demanded. Nor did he want to leave the comfort and love of his Father to go to hell to take the keys of death away from Satan. He knew it was God's plan but the reality of all he would have to endure, overcame him.

This would be his greatest triumph but for a moment in time, it was more than he could bear. He sweat blood; he cried; he prayed for God to take this job away from him. But God demanded obedience from Jesus. The plan was in place and Jesus knew that the sacrifice he had already done would not take the place of his obedience to compete his "destiny". He must surrender his will to God's will.

Satan had lied to Jesus. He had tempted Jesus continually through his entire ministry. Satan had offered him an earthly kingdom but Jesus knew he had a godly kingdom. Why settle for less? He would not settle and he would complete his destiny.

Was there a dark time when Jesus felt overwhelmed and he could have accepted Satan's lies? Yes, but, Jesus knew that the plan was to defeat the darkness and allow God to "light" the way for him. To do this, he would have to be obedient, and it would lead to his greatest sacrifice. The ultimate sacrifice that would provide humanity with eternal life.

Certainly, we cannot compare our caverns of darkness, our despair or our sacrifices to Jesus', but he showed us the way to the keys of God's kingdom. He set the example for us to follow. We are not any better than him and we must make the sacrifices God has called us to and be obedient to our destiny. Sacrifices will never pay the price for obedience. Obedience is the major KEY to living the life on earth God has called us to and living the kingdom life that Jesus told us about. God expects us to fight the good fight. Never believing Satan's lies over God's truths.

> *"And that about wraps it up. God is strong, and he wants you strong. So take everything the Master has set out for you, well-made weapons of the best materials. And put them to use so you will be able to stand up to everything the Devil throws your way. This is no afternoon athletic contest that we'll walk away from and forget about in a couple of hours. This is for keeps, a life-or-death fight to the finish against the Devil and his angels." Ephesians 6:10-12*

What had Satan lied to me about that completely had me derailed all those months?

1. Time and Age - It is too late to make a difference...I'm too old!
2. Purification – Process of Sin had stolen my life and joy.
3. Redeeming – God can't use me any longer and I'm not redeemable.
4. Love – It was not available to me and I was doomed to be lonely.
5. Fruitless – All the seeds I planted were fruitless and would not produce what I needed. (Law of sowing and reaping)
6. Covenant Relationship - My covenant is in jeopardy.
7. Humility – Pride comes before a fall so I must be walking in pride.
8. Wisdom and Knowledge – God is not giving me the wisdom and knowledge I need to overcome, so I am defeated.
9. Anointing – I have lost my ability to walk in the Spirit

Fear was the result and kingdom life is the solution!

All the things I was struggling with were lies. God was not finished with me. His plan was just beginning, although my earthly years and my experiences of life were many. He would use it all to refine me into the person he intended me to be before the beginning of time, before I was conceived, before I was born.

> *"Jesus said, 'I am the Bread of Life. The person who aligns with me hungers no more and thirsts no more, ever. I have told you this explicitly because even though you have seen me in action, you don't really believe me. Every person the Father gives me eventually comes running to me. And once that person is with me, I hold on and don't let go. I came down from heaven not to follow my own whim but to accomplish the will of the One who sent me.*
>
> *This, in a nutshell, is that will: that everything handed over to me by the Father be completed – not a single detail missed – and at the wrap-up of time I have everything and everyone put together, upright and whole. This is what my Father wants: that anyone who sees the Son and trusts who he is and what he does and then aligns with him will enter real life, eternal life. My part is to put them on their feet alive and whole at the completion of time'." John 6:35-40*

When we are in the test, it is so hard not to doubt God and his promises. It is so easy to wonder why God is not hearing our cries for help. Has he forgotten me or just too busy with someone else? No! God always hears us and he will never break even one single promise that is in his Word.

The trial of our faith is the test of a lifetime. We are put here on earth for the purpose of refining our character and letting God show us his character through us. And as that occurs, we are continually moving from one level of glory to another.

What does that mean? That means he wants us to face our situations like he would. He wants us to face difficulties with a heart of praise and "count it all JOY!" No matter what we are going through, we must always believe it is impossible for God to break his word. We must understand that there are just going to be times of testing. That doesn't mean they get any easier but it does mean that God is in control and will walk with us through the test.

It would be nice if we never had to deal with our emotions during the testing. They get us in trouble every time. God has not made us to be like robots and only do as he says, but he made us to have constructive thoughts, feelings and emotions that we must work through and learn to control in godly ways. Also, he gave us freewill to make choices. During these tests, our emotions try to overpower our spiritual logic, which allows our feelings to replace the powerful Word of God.

It is easy to feel we have a right to our feelings, but God said our soul is where the battle begins through our emotions. He tells us to *"Count it all joy" (James 1:2)*. Can we have negative feelings about our trials and test, and just feel sorry for ourselves? No, it says "count it all joy" not "count some as joy".

To some, this just doesn't seem logical. But it doesn't matter! God's Word says

> *"...we know that all things work together for good to them that love God, to them who are the called according to his purposes." Romans 8:28, KJ*

God allows these tests to prepare us for promotion and to show the Devil that we have developed godly character. And like Job (who God considered as an excellent example of godly man) was tested, so God will allow Satan to test us to prove our loyalty to his principles. Satan was allowed to test Job in every area of his live: his family, his business and his health; but he was not allowed to take Job's life. And there was one moment that all of it paid off when Job proved he was truly a righteous man of God. He never denied God and he continually blessed him; because he knew that he was called of God and that all things would work for good in his life.

There is transforming power when our minds are renewed by God's Word. When we are so submitted to God and believe his Word to the point that our emotions no longer matter and have no power over us. At that point, we cease to be victims of our emotions and we realize it is more important for us to be in God's plan and his will. If we are kicking, yelling and pitching a fit and allowing emotions to control us, it is a sign that we are not yet submitted to God and that we are not trusting him to make all things good for us.

So are you trusting God when it really gets tough? Are you going from glory to glory and showing more of a godly character like Job? We should....

> *"Consider it a sheer gift, friends, when tests and challenges come at you from all sides. You know that under pressure, your faith-life is forced into the open and shows its true colors. So don't try to get out of anything prematurely. Let it do its work so you become mature and well-developed, not deficient in*

any way. ... Anyone who meets a testing challenge head-on and manages to stick it out is mighty fortunate. For such persons loyally in love with God, the reward is life and more life." James 1:2-4, 12

"Don't let anyone under pressure to give in to evil say, 'God is trying to trip me up.' God is impervious to evil, and puts evil in no one's way. The temptation to give in to evil comes from us and only us. We have no one to blame but the leering, seducing flare-up of our own lust. Lust gets pregnant, and has a baby. SIN! Sin grows up to adulthood, and becomes a real killer...

So, my very dear friends, don't get thrown off course. Every desirable and beneficial gifts comes out of heaven. The gifts are rivers of light cascading down from the Father of Light. There is nothing deceitful in God, nothing two-faced, nothing fickle. He brought us to life using the true Word, showing us off as the crown of all his creatures." James 1:13-15, 16-18.

Is it possible to live a perfect life? In James 1:4 it states, *"But let patience have her perfect work, that you may be perfect and entire, wanting nothing." (King James).* We all go through tests to move us toward perfection. But notice, it uses the word "PATIENCE". To be patient is one of the hardest things for humans to do and it is even harder to understand the complete meaning of waiting when the pain is so great.

When we are in the "hottest battles" of the test, the Holy Word reminds us we are in the hands of God and it is his job *to put us on our feet alive and whole at the completion of time. John 6:40.* But when God is allowing our character to be tested, it seems that time moves at a snail's pace. The endurance itself is a trial of our patience and it seems so terrific at the time that we, in the natural, fight for survival.

Until it brings us to the death of ourselves, we do not become alive in God. We don't always know what God has in mind for us during the trial. But, if we remain in a state of trust and pliable in his hands, he will craft the most perfect person and life that we could ever imagine with nothing lacking.

God tells us: *"Up on your feet! Go to the potter's house. When you get there, I'll tell you what I have to say. So I went to the potter's house, and sure enough, the potter was there, working away at his wheel. Whenever the pot*

> *the potter was working on turned out badly, as sometimes happens when you are working with clay, the potter would simply start over and use the same clay to make another pot." Jeremiah 18:1-4*

The potter is God and we are the clay. God makes us a perfect vessel; but things happen or our will takes us down the wrong path. Instead of throwing us away, God will put us back on the potter's wheel and start to re-fashion us again into the vessel he designed us to be.

> *"Can't I do just as this potter does, people of Israel? At any moment I may decide to pull up a people...But if they repent of their wicked lives, I will think twice and start over with them...But if they don't cooperate and won't listen to me, I will think again and give up on the plan I had for them...Turn back from your doomed way of life. Straighten out your lives." Jeremiah 18:6-8, 10-11*

As the potter can give up on the clay vessel, God can too...but that is not his desire. He wants to work with us over and over again until we are complete. Until he can look at us and know we have been changed and willing to do what his plan for us is...OUR DESTINY!

To be complete means not being moved by anything of the earthly world but to be living in God's divine peace that the "true" Kingdom of God provides. We then don't care about our earthly desires. Our character then becomes identical to Jesus' who wants only the thoughts and desires of his heavenly Father; so that we may be perfect and complete, lacking nothing.

So with patience, it would be nice to have a little wisdom. If you do not know what to do to sustain the attitude of patience, ask God for wisdom.

> *"Don't bargain with God. Be direct. Ask for what you need. This isn't a cat-mouse, hide-and seek game we're in. If your child asks for bread, do you trick him with sawdust? If he asks for fish, do you scare him with a live snake on his plate? As bad as you are, you wouldn't think of such a thing. You're at least decent to your own children. So don't you think the God who conceived you in love will be even better?" Matthew 7:7-11*

Wisdom to have patience is a good gift that God your father loves to give. With wisdom and faith in God, we will have all we need to stand through the toughest of times and see the completion of our character to another level of glory and to eventual perfection. If we ask, God will always give us wisdom and gives it to us freely without limitation. And we must have faith to believe in the wisdom he gives. Without believing and applying faith, we cannot please God. This leads us into new areas of the kingdom life!

> *"Start with God—the first step in learning is bowing down to God; only fools thumb their noses at such wisdom and learning. Play close attention, friend, to what your father tells you; never forget what you learned." Proverbs 1:7*

God does not honor unbelief; he honors faith in the truth. How do you know if you are walking in faith? We must be careful. One sure sign of unbelief is asking multiple times just for the sake of asking for the same thing; therefore, revealing your unbelief. God has the abundance to meet every need and he knows very well when you don't trust him to meet your need and so you don't get what you're asking for.

God wants more than anything for us to trust him and to stay away from the mind game of testing him with our unbelief. We must get to a place of knowing him and trusting him and believing:

> *"It's impossible to please God apart from faith. And why? Because anyone who wants to approach God must believe both that he exists and that he cares enough to respond to those who seek him." Hebrews 11:6*

Are you at that place where God can promote you in your trial? Do you dare to trust God to get you to a place of <u>No</u> complaints; <u>No</u> crying; <u>No</u> telling everyone about your trial? Another way we prove that we are trusting God for victory is by thanking him for the tests and the results you are going to have at the end. That shows God that we are being patient to keep believing, and not fearing but walking in faith to the end.

And don't think you will not be tempted during the trial. (Let's re-read what James said!)

> *"Don't let anyone under pressure to give in to evil say, 'God is trying to trip me up.' God is impervious to evil, and puts evil in no one's way. The temptation to give in to evil comes from us and only us. We have no one to*

blame but the leering, seducing flare-up of our own lust. Lust gets pregnant, and has a baby. SIN! Sin grows up to adulthood, and becomes a real killer...

So, my very dear friends, don't get thrown off course. Every desirable and beneficial gift comes out of heaven. The gifts are rivers of light cascading down from the Father of Light. There is nothing deceitful in God, nothing two-faced, nothing fickle. He brought us to life using the true Word, showing us off as the crown of all his creatures." James 1:13-18

All unbelief is sin and without faith we cannot please God. Therefore, there is no victory until our faith is tested to this degree. The "Rivers of Light" that I had been seeking is found in the "Father of Light", God himself!

Satan had filled me full of lies but the truth was that God had set me free from Satan's lies with the truth of his Word as I walk in his kingdom principles. God is light and there is always a light at the end of the tunnel. There is an end to the testing and the glory of God will be revealed!

Kingdom Thinking

What lies has Satan been feeding you? Add to the list other lies of Satan you have experienced in your life.

Have you ever been in a cavern like the author described? Give a brief description of how you felt.

Give an example of a time that your emotions took over your faith during the trail.

What words of wisdom in this chapter hit home for you today? How has this changed your prospective of testing?

Keys to the Kingdom

- God requires obedience over sacrifice.
- Satan is a "Liar", seeking to build fear in us.
- We cannot please God without faith.
- Testing is part of kingdom life.
- God gives wisdom without limit.
- Unbelief is sin.
- We will be tempted during the trials.
- God requires us to be patient.
- God wants to purify our character and move us from glory to glory.

CHAPTER 5

Kingdom Health Care System

Jesus' Shed Blood

From the time that I was a young child sitting in both the Baptist and Pentecostal churches, I remember hearing the term "The Blood of Jesus". The "blood songs" that were sung each week adding to my knowledge about the blood. Between the preaching and the singing, I always wanted more of Jesus. Songs like "Nothing but the Blood" and "Whiter than Snow" were staples and frequently sung along with many other great hymns songs. They were so uplifting and so powerful.

Times have changed and rarely do we hear these songs that were so loved by previous generations of Christians. Today's churches don't like to talk or sing about the blood of Jesus. They feel it turns non-believers away from the church. Others say it makes the crucifixion much too graphic, and over time, it has become a taboo topic to sing or teach about.

Without having the teachings on the blood and singing the "blood songs", it has taken many years of studying on my own to grasp the knowledge that has been lost and for me to acquire a renewed understanding of how the blood affects our Christian kingdom life. Thank goodness, even though the church stopped teaching about the blood, it did not stop teaching on salvation through Jesus' death on the cross. For without that message, church as we know it would have died and they would have just become places where we heard motivational teachings on what a "good man named Jesus" taught about in a book called the Bible. Without the message of the blood of Jesus, we have become churches of salvation minus the power Jesus intended us to walk in when he shed his blood on the cross.

It is at the moment a person accepts Jesus that they are no longer an enemy of God and they become redeemed and righteous. This allows them to have a relationship with God the Father. However, little credit is given to the blood, yet it is the blood of Jesus that washed away the sin that has separated us from God and it the blood that gives us the power to live the life that he planned for us.

> *"Come. Sit down. Let's argue this out." This is Gods' Message: "If your sins are blood-red, they'll be snow-white. If they're red like crimson, they'll be like wool."* *Isaiah 1:18*

Our sins are deep stains and only the blood of Jesus can wash them whiter than snow as if we had never sinned. This is the good news of the Bible and it is the start to our kingdom life!

> *"Saying the welcoming word to God – 'Jesus is my Master' – embracing, body and soul, God's work of doing in us what he did in raising Jesus from the dead. That's it. You're not doing anything, you're simply calling out to God, trusting him to do it for you. That's salvation."* *Romans 10:9*

God's use of the blood for the remission of sin was in his plan before the foundation of the world was in place. He knew that man would fall by committing sin, just as Lucifer had in heaven. So a plan to cleanse our sins was not an afterthought. Before Adam was created, God predestined Jesus' birth so his blood would save not only Adam but all future mankind that wanted fellowship with God the Father. God's plan was

- To make man a spirit in God's image with a body and soul (mind, will and emotions).
- To have fellowship with the Father, mankind would have to be free of sin.
- To have a man that would love God and would want to work with him.
- To let man have full dominion over the works that God created.
- To redeem man when he was tempted for wanting his own will.

But to do this, the man must be created by using God's blood. (Adam's name in Hebrew means "a man of the blood from the ground".) In the Bible, God described the use of blood in creation, which resulted in Jesus' (man's) blood being used for atonement of sin; ensuing God's plan of eternal life.

> *"For the life of an animal (flesh) is in the blood. I have provided the blood for you to make atonement for your lives (souls) on the Altar; it is the blood, the life that makes atonement."* *Leviticus 17:11*

Adam being made from the ground was an earthen vessel that could be broken and the blood poured out (like being cut and bleeding out the wound). Therefore, if Adam's "will" caused him to sin like Lucifer's "will" did, it was God's plan to incarnate a Divine Man (with God the Father's blood running through his veins) who could live a perfect life without sin on earth. Then his blood could be used for the atonement of human man's sin. This led to the divine conception of a man, through Mary, a virgin girl.

> *"Upon entering, Gabriel (An Angel): Good Morning! You're beautiful with God's beauty. Beautiful inside and out! God be with you. She was thoroughly shaken, wondering what was behind a greeting like that. But the angel assured her, Mary, you have nothing to fear. "God has a surprise for you: You will become pregnant and give birth to a son and call his name Jesus. He will be great, be called 'Son of the Highest.' The Lord God will give him the throne of his father David; He will rule Jacob's house forever—no end, ever, to his kingdom."*
>
> *Mary said to the angel, "But how? I've never slept with a man." The angel answered, The Holy Spirit will come upon you, the power of the Highest hover over you; Therefore, the child you bring to birth will be called Holy, Son of God."* Luke 1:35

We don't know how everything happened, but it did and it was done by the Trinity - of Father, Son and Holy Ghost. This was God's great redemption plan. His name was Jesus and in Hebrews 10:7-9, it tells how Jesus responded to God's demand for saving humanity by death on the cross. This was God's will for him:

> *"Jesus said, 'I'm here to do it your way, O God, (God's will) the way it's described in your Book...You don't want sacrifices and offerings,' he was referring to practices according to the old plan. When he added, 'I'm here to do it your way,' he set aside the first in order to enact the new plan."*

In this great redemption plan, God's Son became

> *"...the Lamb slain from the foundation of the world."* Revelation 13:18
>
> *"...He paid with Christ's sacred blood, you know. He died like an unblemished sacrificial lamb. And this was no afterthought. Even though it has only lately—at the end of the ages—become public knowledge, God always knew he was going to do this for you."* 1 Peter 1:19-20

The lambs of the Old Testament were replaced with the new Lamb slain from the foundation of the world, JESUS.

Salvation is not the only reason Jesus shed his blood; however without it, there is little hope for our lives to become any better. Out of his death and the shedding of his blood, come more results. The second half of God's plan for us is to live full of joy, peace and happiness. This is also done through Jesus' blood. He not only saves you from sin, but he continues to save you.

What all does that include? The following is not an inclusive list but are some of the most important areas that God wants us to be saved from!

FORGIVENESS

Just because we are saved when we confess with our mouth the Lord Jesus is our Savior, it does not mean we will never sin again. In fact, the Bible states that if you say you don't sin, then God calls you a liar. We all sin! The word "saved" in the original Greek language is *"sozo"* which means to be completely whole. Having salvation from our sin includes receiving everything that is ours which was purchased by the blood of Jesus.

Another thing it means is ongoing forgiveness from our daily sins. We want to continually have a relationship with God the Father; so we must have continual forgiveness for ongoing sin to have that relationship; therefore,

> *"... if we admit our sins—make a clean breast of them—he won't let us down; he'll be true to himself. He'll forgive our sins and purge us of all wrong doing."* 1 John 1:9

We must continue to confess our sins and Jesus will be faithful to continue to forgive us by covering us with the blood he shed. Being saved is an ongoing action, repeating the action each time we let ourselves sin as a result of the fallen sinful world we live in.

OVERCOMING SIN DAILY

God wants to do far more for us than saving us and forgiving us. He wants us to be conquerors over the power of sin. It is our job after salvation to realistically assess our abilities to overcome all that Satan will be trying to do to destroy us and make us less than God's purposes for us. Each person has their own strengths and weaknesses according to the set of talents we inherited from God. Those talents plus our earthly experiences and the lessons we have learned through them, affect how we will fight the battle of sin in our lives. It isn't long after salvation that we realize that the cards are stacked against us and we need more help than our own strength and abilities to become an overcomer and conqueror. We soon turn to God and ask for his help and he starts showing us his truths that will set us free. The shed blood of Jesus becomes a source of power, no matter how big the problem or strong the evil attack.

When life is at its worst and it looks like in our own strength we will lose the battle, all we have to do is call on Jesus and the blood that saves us and claim his promises.

> *"Do you think anyone is going to be able to drive a wedge between us and Christ's love for us? There is no way! Not trouble, not hard times, not hatred, not hunger, not homelessness, not bullying threats, not backstabbing, not even the worst sins listed in Scripture...None of this fazes us because Jesus loves us. I'm absolutely convinced that nothing—nothing living or dead, angelic or demonic, today or tomorrow. High or low, thinkable—unthinkable--absolutely nothing can get between us and God's love because of the way that Jesus our Master has embraced us." Romans 8:35-39*

Satan is roaring in your ears when circumstances seem to spell defeat. Satan tries to keep you beaten down by telling you, you are going to lose the battle. But Satan is not going to win, because you were made to win, if you faint not and claim you are more than a conqueror. The spirit within you must proclaim, "In the name of Jesus and by the power of his blood, I will win the battle." Then victory will be yours!

We must remember that Satan doesn't give up, so how can we. We are warriors and Jesus has the final say. We are on the winning side. Our enemy attacks our mind, body and our emotions but the spirit within us is stronger if we endure to the end. Remember, Satan is accusing us before the throne of God both day and night and when it is our turn to defend ourselves to God, we just have to claim "not guilty" because Jesus defeated Satan on the cross. We are set free by the blood he shed and when he said, *"IT IS FINISHED" (John 19:30).* We as believers now have a blood covenant between us and God. *"We are Overcomers by the Blood of the Lamb and the word of our testimony". Revelation 12:11*

CROSSING OVER INTO THE KINGOM OF GOD

TO HEALTH AND PROSPERITY

We have all heard the story of Jesus going to the cross. Most of us have read and studied the New Testament where the word "cross" is used 28 times and in each of the four gospels, Matthew, Mark, Luke and John which, tell "The Crucifixion Story". Books are written and movies have been made that go into great graphic detail of the horrible, brutal beating the Romans gave our Lord before he died. On Easter Sunday every year, every Christian church's sermon tells the story to remind us of God's love for us...that he gave his only son to save us from our sins. The story never gets old; each time we hear it, we learn a little more of what all Jesus accomplished that day for us to use in our daily life. God's plan was multi-faceted and it is our responsibility to find out all the facets that we have available to us. A majority of the time the presenter/speaker falls short of telling the depth of all that was accomplished for us.

The most important part is that we were forgiven for our sins and received eternal life as a result of accepting Jesus as our savior; but let's go deeper in the provisions it provides us after salvation. Let's look at what it means to share the kingdom life Jesus foretold to his disciples, that they would receive after his death and ascension into heaven.

I understand that it is important to recognize that our Lord endured far more for us that I could even imagine. However, these cruel and awful details had stopped me from studying the power of the cross and the benefit of his blood for years. I will never forget sitting under one evangelist who was a guest speaker at my home church, who went into such detail about the crucifixion, when my spirit could no longer handle it; I got up and walked out in order to control my emotions. Then, I saw Mel Gibson's movie, "The Passion", where it showed such visual and bloody scenes that I had to keep my eyes shut not to see all the gore. I finally got past all my strong emotions and realized: the story is not the gore but the power of the blood!

It was after a vacation to Orlando, Florida and visiting "The Holy Land Experience", that God put it on my heart to study the crucifixion in more detail. I had attended a "passion play" that had really touched me. Yes, the drama showed Jesus being beaten and his blood shed but it was a tamer version so children and people like me who had a problem with the cruelty could enjoy the story. Not only did God encourage me to study the Scriptures again, but he directed me to paint a picture of it. I am a landscape artist and I hadn't ever painted anything like the vision he gave me to paint.

On a 36"x 24" canvas, I was directed to paint every event of the crucifixion:

- The Garden of Gethsemane with Jesus and his closest disciples: Peter, James and John
- Judas and the soldiers coming to get Jesus
- The city of Jerusalem where Pilate judged Jesus
- The three crosses on the mountain of Golgotha where Jesus was crucified
- The resurrection grave with the attending angel
- Jesus' ascension into heaven
- Jesus coming back in the sky for his second coming.

It took more than a year to get the painting completed but by the time I finished the project, I had a completely new appreciation for what Jesus had done for us.

There was no blood painted in the picture, but God revealed to me a whole different meaning and appreciation of the purposes of Jesus' shed blood.

Jesus shed his blood seven different ways, seven different times. Each of these ways are representative of what the blood can do for us in our daily life, to be overcomers and live prosperous lives in the Kingdom of God.

1. REDEEM YOUR WILLPOWER!

We lost our power over "our will" when Adam sinned in the Garden of Eden and chose to eat of the apple from the Tree of Knowledge of Good and Evil. It is no coincidence that Jesus shed his blood in another garden, the Garden of Gethsemane, the night before he was crucified.

Since Adam made the decision to choose his own will over God's will, humanity has continually fought battles over the power to do what he knows is the will of God. Have you ever heard yourself say, "I have no willpower; I want to stop but I just can't"? Over-eating, controlling our temper, excess drinking and drugs, controlling our thoughts are just a few of the areas man has lost the battle of will power and given it to the enemy. We want to do what is right but we just don't have what it takes to correct our actions. Adam wasn't just sinning when he ate the fruit; he was spiritually saying 'I want my will over yours', God. From that moment on, Adam's disobedience cost him the ability to always say "no" to the temptations of Satan instead of saying "yes" to all the good God intended for him.

In the Garden of Gethsemane, Jesus knew what his accusers were going to do to him. He didn't want to go through all the pain and brutal treatment that he knew was coming. He wanted to find an easier way. But, after an emotional battle to do God's will, his own desires did not stop him from doing what was right...to do the good that God had asked him to do.

> In his body, Jesus faced the same battle that Adam faced... *"He fell on his face, praying, 'Father, remove this cup from me.'* But Jesus fought the battle in the spirit and submitted to God. *'But please, not what I want. What do you want?"* *Luke 22:42-46*

Jesus had to continually fight to do the Father's will. He went three times to his beloved disciples, Peter, James and John to ask them to support him in his battle to do the will of the Father over the will of man. When he turned to God for help, his father helped him by sending an angel for encouragement.

> *"At once an angel from heaven was at his side, strengthening him."* He prayed on all the harder. *"Sweat, wrung from him like drops of blood, poured off his face"...* He returned to his disciples and told them to *'Pray so you won't give in to temptation.'* (Counseling with words of knowledge that they, Peter, James and John would also face the same temptations of their own "will" in their hour of grief.) Luke 22:43-46

Medical doctors have confirmed that at times of great anxiety, human blood vessels can break under the skin and blood will secrete through the pores like sweat. This was the blood that was shed to redeem "our willpower" from submission to Satan and gave us the power to do the will of God. And then Jesus spoke, "Father, not my will but your will." This was his declaration of the power to overcome Satan's temptations.

You can do this, too. You have the choice to use the redeemed blood of Jesus that he shed through his own pores to do God's will. You have the power to overcome those things you didn't think you could and couldn't in yourself; you have the power to proclaim victory over drugs, alcohol, tempers, eating disorders, etc.

What Adam lost in the Garden of Eden was restored in the Garden of Gethsemane. All you have to do is "PLEAD THE BLOOD OF JESUS."

2. REDEEM YOUR HEALTH!

After Jesus agreed with the Father to do his will, Jesus waited in the garden for Judas Iscariot to bring the Roman soldiers to arrest him for conspiracy against the Jewish laws (an accusation that was never proven). During the trial, the Chief Priest asked Jesus if he was the Messiah.

> *"Are you the Messiah, the Son of the Blessed? And Jesus said, 'Yes, I am and you'll see it yourself. The Son of Man seated at the right hand of the Mighty one, arriving on the clouds of Heaven.' The Chief Priest lost his temper. Ripping his clothes, he yelled, "Did you hear that?" After that, do we need witnesses?"* *Mark 14:61-63*

After he later proclaimed again to be Jesus the Son of God, the Chief Priest said;

> *"You heard the blasphemy. Are you going to stand for it?" They condemned him, one and all. The sentence: death."* *Mark 14:63*

Jesus was then turned over to Pilate, who found no guilt in Jesus; therefore, he didn't want to pronounce Jesus guilty of anything. As it was a Jewish custom at Passover to allow the crowd of Jerusalem to determine which of the prisoners they would like to have released during feast days, Pilate hoped they wouldn't choose a murderer instead of Jesus. The High Priest of the city continued to encourage the crowds to release Barabbas, a murder rather than Jesus the King of the Jews. Finally, the crowd repeatedly yelled,

> *..."Nail him to a cross!" Pilate objected, "But for what crime?" But they yelled all the louder, "Nail him to a cross!" Pilate gave the crowd what it wanted, set Barabbas free and turned Jesus over for whipping and crucifixion." Mark 15: Mark 15: 13-15*

It was a custom for all prisoners about to be crucified to first be given 40 lashes in order to weaken their bodies. In the past, many of the criminals died from the lashes alone because it was such a cruel punishment and as a result they cut the number down to 39 lashes because the 40th lash had proven to be the fatal lash. Jesus received 39 which was the custom. It has been said by doctors, that all illness stems from 39 root diseases. Nothing about God's plans is coincidence; there is a reason for everything. Do you suppose that each lash Jesus took on his body represented one of the roots of those diseases? The lashes Jesus took were for our healing.

> *"But it was our sins that did that to him, that ripped and tore and crushed him—our sins! He took the punishment, and that made us whole. Through his bruises we get healed." Isaiah 53:5*

It was original sin that allowed sickness to enter the world but because Jesus died to bring the Kingdom of God to earth, Jesus paid the price not only for our sin but for our health, by taking the whip on his back and shedding his blood.

We do play a major part in our healing. God always requires something from you in order to receive his blessings. You must believe by faith that Jesus did this for you and that each time he was flogged by the whip and his skin and muscles were ripped, it was so you could claim healing. It doesn't matter if it is cancer, a birth defect, injury or a spirit of infirmity, they are all from Satan and Jesus took the stripes on his back in order to heal them all. Nowhere in the Bible does it say that some things or some people were not meant to be healed. No! ALL were to be healed. Re-read Isaiah 53...It was meant for ALL to be whole. This was so important that Peter stated it again in the New Testament.

> *"He (God) used his servant body to carry our sins to the Cross so we could be rid of sin, free to live the right way. His wounds became our healing."* 1 Peter 2:24

It is God's will that we are healed and it is Jesus who paid the price for us to be healed. You must believe and walk confidently in faith in his healing promises. Don't try to understand how it will happen or when it will happen but believe it will happen. Jesus taught us to come to God as a little child trusting your heavenly father to give you his good gifts of kingdom life. Healing is a good gift!

> *"Beloved, I wish above all things that thou mayest prosper and be in health, even as thy soul prospereth."* *3 John 1:2 KJ*

> *"Ask boldly, believing, without a second thought. People who worry their prayers are like wind-whipped waves. Don't think you're going to get anything from the Master that way."."* *James 1:6*

> *"If your child asks for bread, do you trick him with sawdust? If he asks for a fish, do you scare him with a live snake on his plate? As bad as you are, you wouldn't think of such a thing. You're at least decent to your own children. So don't you think the God who conceived you in love will be even better?"* *Matthew 7:9-11*

Jesus took a whipping for our health and all we have to do is "PLEAD THE BLOOD OF JESUS".

3. REDEEM YOUR PROSPERITY!

When Adam and Eve entered the Garden of Eden, they lived in perfect peace, health and prosperity, wanting nothing. But when they sinned and disobeyed God, everything changed. God actually cursed the land that he had created. God told Adam:

> *"Because you listened to your wife and ate from the tree that I commanded you not to eat from, 'Don't eat from this tree,' the ground is cursed because of you; getting food from the ground will be painful as having babies is for your wife, you'll be working in pain all your life long. The ground will sprout thorns and weeds, you'll get*

> *your food the hard way, planting and tilling and harvesting, sweating in the fields from dawn to dusk, until you return to that ground yourself, dead and buried, you started out as dirt, you'll end up dirt."* Genesis 3:17-19

It was not until Jesus had a crown made from a thorn bush placed on his head and his shed blood ran down his brow, that this curse was reversed. It was this curse which changed paradise into a desert land; lacking all the blessings God intended for man to enjoy in a land of plenty. Man would now have to work to survive. It was thorns and weeds, a symbol of poverty, from the ground that the soldiers cut and formed into the crown that caused redemption of the land. Instead of sweat pouring out, blood poured out and that blood can now be claimed to regain prosperity instead of poverty.

> *"You are familiar with the generosity of our Master, Jesus Christ. Rich as he was, he gave it all away for us—in one stroke he became poor and we became rich."* 2 Corinthians 8:9

Jesus paid the price for us to redeem prosperity and all that we had lost in the Garden of Eden. He left the riches of heaven and came to earth for a short period of time so that we could reclaim the riches of the land. Satan tells us the lie—that Jesus was poor, so what do we think? We think we should not desire riches while we are on the earth. The true answer to that question is that Jesus shed his blood to help us redeem what was lost through Adam's sin. Adam lost his prosperity, but we can regain ours through the blood of Jesus.

Jesus himself told a parable about being the gate for his sheep and the sheep will know his voice. When the people of his day did not understand the parable, He explained its meaning. Satan was the stranger who entered into the sheep's pen through the fence, not through the gate, and since he was not the shepherd, the sheep did not recognize his voice and would not follow him. The result was the sheep did not trust him. Jesus describes the stranger as being a thief and says:

> *"A thief is only there to steal and kill and destroy. I came so they can have real and eternal life, more and better life than they ever dreamed of. I am the Good Shepherd. The Good Shepherd puts the sheep before himself, sacrifices himself if necessary."* John 10:10-11

This was a warning that Satan is a thief who only wants to steal, kill and destroy Jesus' believers. Jesus, the "good" shepherd wants us to be attentive to his voice and only obey and trust him. One of Satan's biggest lies (that God doesn't want us to believe) is that we should live in lack or poverty. God originally meant for us to have everything that we wanted and needed. It was only because of Adam's sin, that God cursed the ground. To restore prosperity to the land, God sent his son to die for us and redeem all that Satan stole. It is up to you to claim the abundant life and not buy in to Satan's lie that poverty is part of the original curse. The curse was that we would have to toil and work hard to just get our needs met. But, because of the redemption Jesus provided when he shed his precious blood as the crown of thorns was placed on his head, we have God's renewed desire for us to be prosperous.

Man has come to believe that only in our own power can wealth be obtained, but Moses reminded the Israelites that it is God who gives us the ability to obtain prosperity.

> *"If you start thinking to yourselves, "I did all this. And all by myself. It's all mine.'—well think again.*
>
> *Remember that God, your God, gave you the strength to produce all this wealth so as to confirm the covenant that he promised to your ancestors..." Deuteronomy 8:17-18.*

And Solomon said:

> *"A good life gets passed on to the grandchildren; ill-gotten wealth ends up with good people." Proverbs 13:22*

Prosperity is part of God's redemptive plan for his people. God can multiply our work efforts to accomplish in a month what takes the sinner years to do. In fact, God says, in the last days he will even transfer the wealth of the sinners to his believers. "The wealth of the sinners is stored up for the righteous." Proverbs 13:22 KJ

Jesus wears a crown in heaven made of jewels but when he was on earth, he wore a crown of thorns so we could live a life of prosperity. All you have to do is "PLEAD THE BLOOD OF JESUS".

4. REDEEMED YOUR DOMINION OVER THE EARTH!

When God created the earth, he thought of everything that man would need: food, water, shelter and relationship. He wanted Adam to want nothing but to have a source for meeting every need. When man was created, he didn't know what he would need to survive but he had nothing to worry about. Why? Because God thought of it all. I believe that even the weather was a perfect temperature for Adam's comfort. God even considered the need of water for the plants, animals and man and he supplied it every night with the dew.

> *"He causeth vapours to ascend from the ends of the earth; he maketh lightnings for the rain, he bringeth the wind out of his treasuries."*
>
> *Psalms 135:7 KJ*

All the problems came about as a result of the fall of man! When Adam sinned, it allowed Satan to introduce all the bad things we now have--the opposite of what God intended for good. God made everything perfect with nothing lacking while Satan destroyed. He stole the perfection and peace that God intended for man and replaced it with the negative and destructive things we now experience in our world.

Not only was everything perfect that he created, but God created it all for Adam's use and for Adam to have dominion over while he was on the earth.

> *God spoke: "Let us make human beings in our image, make them reflecting our nature so they can be responsible for the fish in the sea, the birds in the air, the cattle, and, yes, Earth itself, and every animal that moves on the face of Earth." God created human beings; he created them godlike, reflecting God's nature. He created them male and female.*
>
> *God blessed them: "Prosper! Reproduce! Fill Earth! Take Charge!"* (Have Dominion--KJ) *"Be responsible for fish in the sea and birds in the air, for every living thing that moves on the face of Earth"*
>
> *Then God said, "I've given you every sort of seed-bearing plant on Earth and every kind of fruit bearing tree, given them to you for food. To all animals and all birds, everything that moves and breathes, I give whatever grows out of the ground for food."*

> *And there it was. God looked over everything he had made; it was so good, so very good! Genesis 1:26-31*

God gave Adam dominion and authority over it all! But when Adam sinned, it so displeased God that everything changed. The authority was no longer Adam's but Satan's and he took control and became the god (little "g") of the earth. God didn't give it to Satan. Because of Adam's choice to follow Satan's lie, he relinquished it over to Satan. All of this happened because Adam ate a piece of fruit from the Tree of Knowledge of Good and Evil. Adam made Satan his "god", and authority over the earth became his. Humanity has been battling for that control ever since.

But God had a plan to overcome all that Satan meant for bad. His name was Jesus, the second Adam, and his destiny was to redeem all that the first Adam had lost in the Garden of Eden. Jesus laid his life down in order to save us and restore the authority back to us. He not only laid his life down but he laid his body down without a battle on the cross and allowed the soldiers to drive the spikes into his hands. It is hard for us to understand... that once Jesus won the battle of God's will over his own will in the Garden of Gethsemane, he relinquished even his emotions and fear of the pain that he would have to face.

How do we know that?

- He didn't fight when the soldiers came to arrest him!
- He didn't fight to win over the high priest's arguments of guilt in Pilate's court!
- He didn't fight with the Jews to choose him over Barabbas to be released!
- He didn't fight when they stripped his clothes off him and put a crown of thorns on his head!
- He didn't fight when they tied him to the whipping post!
- He didn't fight the soldiers when they forced him to carry his cross up the mountain of Golgotha!
- He didn't fight when they forced him to lie down on the wood of the cross in order to nail his hands and feet to the cross!

He didn't fight because he knew it was his destiny to die for you and me on that cross. To save us from ourselves and from Satan's will to overtake us. Man has come to believe that only in our own power can wealth be obtained, but Moses reminded the Israelites that it is God who gives us that ability to obtain prosperity. Jesus claimed that authority over us and said:

> *"They shall take snakes in their hands, they will drink poison and not be hurt, they will lay hands on the sick and make them well."* *Mark 16:18*

That means that you would be able to take authority over evil and sickness by claiming Jesus's authority and by laying on of hands for other's redemption.

God wants everything we put our hands to, to prosper. God wants us to have dominion over everything on the earth. All we have to do is "PLEAD THE BLOOD OF JESUS".

Kingdom Thinking

What two things that happen at the moment of Salvation?

How did God's Plan of redemption work, utilizing divine blood?

Jesus shed his blood seven different ways, seven different times. Each of these ways are representative of what the blood can do for us in our daily life, to be overcomers and live prosperous lives in the kingdom of God. Can you name the things listed in this chapter that were redeemed?

How did Jesus relinquish his emotions and fear of pain after his experience in the Garden of Gethsemane when he decides he would do God's will not his own?

Keys to the Kingdom

- God's use of the blood for the remission of sin was in his plan before the foundation of the world was in place.
- It was God's plan to incarnate a Divine Man (with God the Father's blood running through his veins) who could live a perfect life without sin on earth. Then his blood could be used for the atonement of humanity's sin.
- The lambs of the Old Testament were replaced with the new Lamb, slain from the foundation of the world, JESUS. The old covenant ended and the new covenant was put in place with Jesus' death on the cross.
- One of the benefits of salvation is the ongoing forgiveness of our sins. If we continue to confess our sins, Jesus will be faithful to continue to forgive us by covering us with the blood he shed.
- Remember, Satan is accusing us before the throne of God both day and night and when it is our turn to defend ourselves to God, we just have to claim "not guilty" because Jesus defeated Satan on the cross.
- Jesus taught us to come to God as a little child trusting our heavenly Father to give us his good gifts of kingdom life, healing, and prosperity!
- Man has come to believe that only in our own power can wealth be obtained, but Moses reminded the Israelites that it is God who gives us that ability to obtain prosperity.

CHAPTER 6

Kingdom Health Care System

Redemption of Fear and Terror

When Adam and Eve realized that they had betrayed their God, fear filled them. They realized that they were naked and were ashamed (a form of terror) and hid from God. They not only lost their dominion over the earth and everything in it, but they lost their peace and they feared how God would respond to their actions. Because they ate from the Tree of Knowledge of Good and Evil, their eyes were opened to evil and they realized that Satan had deceived them.

> *The serpent was clever, more clever than any wild animal that GOD had made. He spoke to the Woman: "Do I understand that God told you to eat from any tree in the garden?" The woman said to the serpent, "Not at all. We can eat from the trees in the garden. It's only the tree in the middle of the garden that God said, 'Don't eat from it; don't even touch it or you'll die.'*
>
> *The serpent told the Woman, "You won't die. God knows that the moment you eat from that tree, you'll see what's really going on. You'll be just like God, knowing everything, ranging all the way from good to evil." When the Women saw that the tree looked like good eating and realized what she would get out of it—she'd know everything! She took and ate the fruit and then gave some to her husband, and he ate. Immediately the two of them did "see what's really going on"—saw themselves naked! They sewed fig leaves together as makeshift clothes for themselves.*
>
> *When they heard the sound of GOD strolling in the garden in the evening breeze, the Man and his Wife hid in the trees of the garden, hid from GOD." Genesis 3:1-10*

I'm sure at that very moment, Adam and Eve wished they could do "a do over". But they could not and therefore, they paid a heavy price for it. They were expelled from the garden and cast out into a place of no godly protection; a land full of "thistles and thorns". A place where they would have to battle extreme environmental changes. They were no longer protected; Adam had given Satan his dominion and authority over the earth.

Man would now face:

- Wild animals: lions, bears and sharks
- Extreme weather: rainstorm, hurricanes and droughts
- Extreme temperatures: freezes and heat waves
- Unusual topography: volcanos and earthquakes

God didn't mean for all these to be harmful and possibly even kill us. He intended for us to have authority over all things that he had provided. The fall of man into sin allowed Satan to introduce the extremes for man to face and try to conquer in his own strength.

God doesn't want us to walk in fear and terror. He meant for man to have authority over all the earth. Everything was placed on earth for our enjoyment. Worrying whether wild animals would cause man harm or whether the earth would shake and collapse under his feet was not God's original plan...God did not want people to be in fear for their life. Many people today live in such fear, that they are afraid to leave their homes and have become reclusive trying to make sure nothing will happen to them and their families.

God was patient, waiting over four thousand years for him to birth Jesus, and for Jesus to mature into an adult man, showing the world that he could withstand temptation and sin. This prepared the way for the Kingdom of God to arrive on Earth again. Through Jesus' shed blood, we can take authority over fear and terror in order to have peace and tranquility over the elements of the earth.

When Jesus started his ministry, he commanded us by saying,

> *"Time's up! God's kingdom is here. Change your life and believe the Message." Mark 1: 15* And at the end of his ministry he commanded us to *"... 'Go into the world. Go everywhere and announce the Message of God's good news to one and all.'" Mark 16:15*

Where did God tell us to go? INTO ALL THE WORLD! Who did God say to give his message to? EVERYONE!

In the fallen state that the world was now in; it would have been almost impossible to fulfill Jesus' command if God did not provide a way for man to reclaim dominion and authority over this earth. God intends for us to have the authority to take the land just as he told the Israelites when he said,

> *"Every square inch on which you place your foot will be yours...No one (or thing) will be able to stand in your way. Everywhere you go, God-sent fear and trembling will precede you, just as he promised."*
> *Deuteronomy 11:24-25.*

Wherever you go, you can have that kind of authority because of the shed blood that flowed out of Jesus' feet. As a result, you can walk safely to spread Jesus' good news: that he came to earth to bring the Kingdom of God. You are to use this power and authority to be strong and exhibit courage; not to be afraid or terrified. Claim your position in Jesus Christ as you face the wiles of the devil, who will try to stop you from doing what God has destined you to do.

As a believer, you can overcome all the fear and terror that Satan tries to use to make you question God's love and his provision for you. You can claim authority and safety over your family, your homes, your communities and your travels.

Every place you put the soles of your feet, you have the victory! How?
Just "PLEAD THE BLOOD OF JESUS"!

5. Redeemed A Life of Joy

Have you ever seen someone die and had the thought that they didn't die from a disease or old age; that they died from a broken heart? I have. My mother-in-law had three children. The last 20 years of her life, I talked with her many times and she expressed how her heart hurt because she could not have her three children together in the same room for dinner or a celebration. Old hurts and differences of opinions had distanced the three siblings from each other. Even though each had a relationship with Mom, her heart was to share family time with all at the same time. One of the girls lived out of town and would come to town once a year and Mom would always try to have a family dinner, to no avail.

After the visits, I noticed she was always depressed or sick. Once she even went to the hospital with a heart problem that the doctors couldn't explain. I believe it was a broken heart.

Jesus experienced these same kinds of feelings during the last days of his life on earth. He had a broken heart because of the betrayal and rejection he experienced from his followers and those he came to personally love.

Who betrayed him?

- Judas, one of the original twelve disciples, turned him over to Roman authorities for gold coins.
- People, who he had blessed, prayed for and healed during his 3 years of ministry, rejected him.
- Many of his followers cried out for Barabbas to be released, instead of Jesus.
- Pilate allowed his crucifixion, even when he felt the witness of the Holy Spirit of Jesus' innocence. Even his wife advised him to let Jesus go after having a dream of Jesus being a just man.
- Peter denied him three times and said he didn't know him!

How was Jesus rejected and humiliated?

- Placed a cruel Crown of Thorns on his head to mock him as the King of the Jews.
- His clothes were torn off him and they were raffled off to soldiers.
- Hung on the cross naked in front of his mother.
- People spit on him as he carried the cross to Golgotha.
- Every sin that had been committed came on him who had never sinned.
- And the worst rejection was his Father, God, had no choice but to turn his back on Jesus as he was covered with the sins of the world.

Jesus showed his extreme feeling of rejection by crying out,

> *"...Eloi, Eloi, lama sabachthani: which means, 'My God, my God, why have you abandoned me?'" Matthew 4:46*

Yes, our Lord and Savior cried with a broken heart on the cross, so YOUR heart could be made whole when his was broken. Every one of us has experienced a broken heart at one time or another. My heart is breaking now as I write this, that Jesus had to experience such severe rejection...but God made a way for all to be healed of broken hearts!

> *"He'll wipe every tear from their eyes. Death is gone for good—tears gone, crying gone, pain gone—all the first order of things gone." Revelation 21: 4*
>
> *"He heals the broken and bandages their wounds." Psalms 147: 3*

Jesus didn't die an ordinary death. Nothing about the entire crucifixion was normal. Most crucified people died one of two ways. Either they died in a very short period of time (a few minutes) or it would take an extended long period of several days. Either way, it usually ended in suffocation when the weight of their body would cause the lungs to collapse. Jesus did not die quickly. He had several conversations while he hung on the cross. One was with John, to take care of his mother. The other with the thief on the cross next to him, where he accepted Jesus as his savior and Jesus told him he would see him in paradise.

Because it was Passover Feast Sabbath, the soldiers were ordered to break the legs of all the prisoners who were still alive so they could be buried before night fall. When they came to Jesus, he was surprisingly already dead. They did not break a single bone, causing fulfillment of the prophecy stated in John 19:36 and Psalms 34:20:

> *"These things that happened confirmed the Scripture, 'Not a bone in his body was broken'."*

Jesus didn't die from suffocation like most others who were sentenced to death by means of crucifixion. Most theologians believe that he died of a broken heart. When the weight of man's sin was laid on him, God had to turn away from that sin, causing Jesus to experience for the first time being rejected by his Father. When they found him dead, the soldiers were surprised because he never showed signs of suffocation. To make sure he was dead, they pierced his heart with a spear and blood and water poured out of the wound.

Jesus died of a broken heart so he could heal ours. He had announced the beginning of his ministry in the Jewish synagogue just three years before by reading Isaiah 61:1-3:

> *"The spirit of God, the Master, is on me because God anointed me. He sent me to preach the good news to the poor, **heal the heartbroken**, announce freedom to all captives, pardon the prisoners.*
>
> *God sent me to announce the year of his grace—a celebration of God's destruction of our enemies—and to comfort all who mourn, to care for the needs of all who mourn in Zion, give them bouquets of roses instead of ashes, **messages of joy** instead of news of doom, a praising heart instead of a languid spirit. Rename them "Oaks of Righteousness" planted by God to display his glory."*

God had a plan for everything to be redeemed that had been lost because of the original sin in the Garden of Eden. Adam and Eve lost their "joy" when they saw how much they had hurt God and broken their fellowship with the God of the universe. They would have consequences for their rejection of God's plan for them. And eventually they would become bitter and would lose their joy and happiness.

But Jesus was sent from God himself, to heal the heartbroken and he gave the oil of joy to those who were mourning! And he proved that those who would partake of his gifts would know,

> ***"The joy of God is your strength!"*** *Nehemiah 8:10.*

The happiness and joy that God had intended for man to have had been stolen by Satan tempting Adam and Eve. With their disobedience, happiness was replaced with feelings of rejection and sadness for disappointing their God. God was not surprised by them choosing to do their own will over his. He knew at some point in time, man would disappoint him so He had designed a plan to restore their joy with a bonus.

When Jesus died on the cross and the soldiers pierced his heart and blood poured out, that blood would redeem the rejection and humiliation of broken hearts to a heart full of joy. Jesus would experience his joy again with the renewed fellowship with God, his Father. Because of Jesus' death and resurrection, not only was a way made for man to be healed but Jesus also experienced new joy and happiness for the broken heart he had experienced because of the rejection and humiliation from those he loved on the earth. The bonus was that God would give Jesus even greater joy for what Satan had robbed from him. In Proverbs 6: 30-31, it explains that when a thief is found, he must restore sevenfold what the person has lost. So, Jesus got the bonus of extreme joy, seven times as much joy when he was restored to his Father. So, when Satan attempts to steal your joy, you can claim a bonus too. You can have seven times as much JOY when you claim the healing for your broken heart.

How do you claim it? By declaring forgiveness to the person who has caused the pain that stole your joy! When you exercise the power of giving your forgiveness to others and receiving forgiveness for your sins from God, you will experience godly freedom, restored confidence and renewed happiness. Every believer is given that power. You have that power! The discovery of that power is life-changing. It drives the devil out of your life and it brings complete joy and peace. God forgives you because he loves you and he was willing to pay the price for your sins with his precious son's death on the cross. Once you have accepted Jesus as your Savior and have experienced new birth, joy will flood you and new hope is experienced. Forgiveness is the source of true happiness. What does God's forgiveness include that gives us a 7 fold reward?

- *He forgives your sins—every one!*
- *He heals your diseases—every one!*
- *He redeems you from hell—saves your life!*
- *He crowns you with love and mercy—a paradise crown!*
- *He wraps you in goodness—eternally!*
- *He renews your youth—you're always young in his presence!*
- *He puts you as a victim back on your feet! Psalms 103:2-6*

How could you not be full of JOY with all of those benefits? As you praise God for these benefits and express how grateful you are for his plan of forgiveness, you will then want to follow the rest of God's requirement for forgiveness. God desires that you then act in love to others, even your enemies. He says you must forgive others if you want him to forgive you. Jesus included this principle of forgiveness twice in the "Lord's Prayer". If it was not important, why did he tell us twice?

"Keep us forgiven with you and forgiving others." Matthew 6:12

AND

> *"In prayer there is a connection between what God does and what you do. You can't get forgiveness from God, without also forgiving others." Matthew 6:14*

Whoa! God put a lot of emphasis on forgiving those who hurt us. He was teaching how to pray but within that teaching, it is as if he stopped and said... 'Listen to what I just said: this will be on the test!' (I know when I taught high school, my students would always take notice when I told them ahead of time; you will be tested on this!).

The opposite of forgiveness is "unforgiveness." Unforgiveness to those who hurt you causes you to hold on to the hurts in your life, which in time will cause you to become bitter if you do not give your hurts to God.

Who wants to **hold on** to their hurts? If you pick up a poisonous snake, do you drop it before it bites you? If you accidently pick up a piece of hot metal, do you think, I know it hurts but why don't I hold on long enough for it to burn me. No! You don't want to hold on to your emotional hurts either. By forgiving the person that hurt you, you are dropping the snake that could kill you or metal that would burn and scar you. Emotional hurts from others without your forgiveness, scar your emotions and changes who you are. Even Jesus while on the cross, had to forgive the ones that hurt him:

> *"Jesus prayed, 'Father, forgive them, they don't know what they're doing'. Dividing up his clothes, they threw dice for them." Luke 23:24*

God didn't design us to carry these emotional toxins in our hearts. He has a better plan. If you will give your hurts to God, he will redeem them and turn them into GOOD! Remember when you walk in forgiveness to those who hurt you, God will forgive you. Then you will be blessed with renewed joy and blessings will reign in your life instead of hate, sadness and bitterness. Jesus' heart was pierced and blood poured out so we could have our broken hearts healed.

Forgiveness will open the door for God to give you greater joy and happiness and it all begins with doing what God has told you to do...forgive others that have broken your heart and "PLEAD THE BLOOD OF JESUS" over them.

6. Redeem Your Inner Healing

The last place that Jesus shed his blood can be found in the following verse.

> *"But he was wounded for our transgressions, he was bruised for our iniquities, the chastisement of our peace was upon him and with his stripes we are healed." Isaiah 53: 5 KJ*

We claim *"he was wounded for our transgressions"* and *"with his stripes we are healed"*... but do we claim, *"he was bruised for our iniquities"?*

Bruises are the seventh way that Jesus shed his blood. We have all bruised our bodies as a result of unusual falls/hits of some kind to our skin or soft body tissues! We really don't realize that the reason for the yellow discoloration of our skin is blood vessels under the skin bursting open and bleeding on the inside of us. So another way of understanding the phrase "bruised for our iniquity" is to understand that God, not only heals us of the outward physical hurts but also of all things that have damaged us in our mind and emotions. Jesus didn't just have physical hurts and wounds, but also had emotional scars and bruises on the inside.

The Romans were brutal when punishing their enemy. They didn't just kill them; they tortured them for days and sometimes years, just to humiliate their victims. They had no shame and no compassion. A physical cut, bruise or sickness is often much less painful to a person than an emotional pain or scar. Others can see the physical injuries and scars, but they do not see the hurts and the emotional scars that individuals also carry. Many of these emotional hurts have tormented them for years. Some people have carried the hurts throughout their entire life as the result of generational curses and even pass them on to the next generation. Doctors say that the physical wounds are much easier to heal than the hidden emotions that have bruised the individual. However, God loves us so much that he wants all of our wounds and sicknesses healed.

The Roman soldiers did enforce the judgments of the Roman authorities by beating and crucifying Jesus, but they were also damaging him at a cellular level.

- Each time they hit him on the outside of his body, the blow would vibrate through his whole body and blood vessels would break in the muscles, tendons and ligaments that could not be seen.
- They said hateful things to him and Jesus many times didn't even respond. *Pilate asked him, "Are you the 'King of the Jews'?" He answered, "If you say so." The high priests let loose a barrage of accusations. Pilate asked again, "Aren't you going to answer anything? That's quite a list of accusations." Still, he said nothing." Mark 15:9-12.* What emotional hurt was he feeling when the high priest of his day rejected and slandered him?
- The rejection he felt from the friends and acquaintances in the crowds as they yelled *"Nail him to a cross." Mark 15:13.* What fear would you have felt if it was you on trial at that moment? Two more times Pilate asked the crowd questions that could have caused him to release Jesus but the crowd responded "Nail him to a cross".

What rejection Jesus must have felt! Rejection causes more emotional trauma than any other emotional response people face. Psychiatrist offices are filled with people who have scars of rejection resulting in a lack of self-confidence—a type of emotional bruising.

"They banged on his head with a club, spit on him, and knelt down in mock worship. After they had had their fun, they took off the purple cape and put his own clothes back on him. Then they marched out to nail him to the cross." Mark 15:19-20. He was attacked both physically and emotionally. How would you have felt if someone spit on you and humiliated you the way his peers did him?

They stripped him of everything:

- *They divided up his clothes and threw dice to see who would get them.*
- *The charge against him-THE KING OF THE JEWS-was printed on a poster that hung over his head.*
- *Along with him, they crucified two criminals, one to his right, the other to his left.*
- *People passing along the road jeered, shaking their heads in mock lament. "You bragged that you could tear down the Temple and then rebuild it in three days—so show us your stuff! Save yourself! If you're really God's Son, come down from that cross!*

- *The high priests, along with the religion scholars, were right there mixing it up with the rest of them, having a great time poking fun at him. "He saved others—but he can't save himself! Messiah, is he? King of Israel? Then let him climb down from that cross. We'll all become believers then!*
- *Even the men crucified alongside him joined in the mockery. Mark 15:24-27, 29-32*
- *The soldiers also came and poked fun of him, making a game of it. They toasted him with sour wine. Luke 23:36*

More rejection and more humiliation! Not only the soldiers but even those who had watched his ministry the last three years, bruised him with their words. The same people who had called him a man of God, a man of integrity, a man that lived a life of purity and humility; tried to strip him of all the good that he had done through rejection and humiliation.

Jesus was physically bruised with the beating but he was emotionally bruised with their words and actions. Both kinds of bruises caused the shedding of Jesus' blood. Both represent what he was willing to go through for our healing.

Many of the psychological bruises we have can be just as life threatening as physical wounds on the outside of us. Let's look at what iniquities are.

> Iniquities are defined as gross injustices or wickedness; violations of the law or rights or duties. They can be wicked acts or unrighteous acts known as sins. These iniquities can be caused by things that we have been involved with or things that our forefathers have passed on to us.

I remember many times, at the end of a church service, the pastor or evangelist that was preaching making the altar call for everyone with a certain illness (such as having heart problems or back pains) to come forward for prayer. There were many times when I wanted to stand up and say... how about people who are hurting inside emotionally? Those people are hurting as much or more than anyone with a physical problem. Years went by with little being mentioned about inner healing for those with hurting souls. I wondered why the church, in general, was more concerned with the physical healing of people than the emotional. It has only been in recent years that the emotional issues have become excessively prevalent and caused the extreme high numbers of suicide and other mental disorders that have plagued our society.

As a result of the emotional stress, alcohol and drug crimes have escalated to such large numbers that our jails and prisons are overflowing with people that are in bondage to them. Murders, robberies, and sexual perversions are a few things that occur as a result of participation in drugs and alcohol or trying to find a way to pay for the habit of the addiction. These two habits (drugs and alcohol) alone change the personalities and core values of the participants, which has caused breakdown of families and has compromised the stability of our society. Many people turn to these substances to ease the pain and problems that were facing them. If we could have helped the people with the problems they were facing before they developed the addiction, a lot of the addiction related issues could have been avoided. It has also been proven that these same cycles continue to their children and others who are caught in the environmental trap of the addict.

This is just an example of one kind of generational curse. The curse, itself, is the demonic force within the person that causes the person harm or destruction. Anger, depression, divorce, suicide/early death in families, poverty, etc. are more examples of inner emotions that need healing to stop the development of generation after generation experiencing the same things over and over again. They act like a fault-line under the surface of the earth, which over time builds up pressure like an earthquake, until it explodes causing devastating results to others.

The people in the destructive pattern wonder why they are like they are or why they keep repeating their actions. They may be born-again Christians who can't understand how they have been set free from lots of other things but cannot get the freedom they need to overcome a particular issue. They are not bad people and many want to please God, but they are still suffering from the iniquity or faults in their soul. The Bible says it this way, *"the truth shall set you free, but if you don't know or realize the truth then lack of knowledge will destroy God's people." Hosea 4:6*

But, God came to heal all emotional problems whether they are old hurts from childhood, a broken marriage or generational curse. The hidden bruises that Jesus suffered during the crucifixion process represents the hidden emotions behind all of our hurts that are so destructive. He took those bruises in order to heal you of your inner hurts. The root of the problem you may be facing today has already been resolved by Jesus and all you have to do is ask God for the TRUTH of why you keep repeating your cycles of hurt over and over again. Don't let Satan's demons destroy you and your family; not your finances, not your willpower, not your health, not your relationships, none have to implode in your life because of a fault you have or curse that has been passed down through your family.

You can have the knowledge you need to confess them to God if you ask him to reveal the source of your problem. Then PLEAD THE BLOOD OF JESUS over you and your family to break any curses that Satan and his demons have placed on you and your family blood line!

God had a plan and Satan had a plan, but God has won the battle over our enemy!

> *"He won't let up until the last enemy is down. He had put all enemies under his feet and the very last enemy that shall be destroyed is death! For he hath put all under his feet..." 1 Corinthians 15:25-27*

God's Healing Power

It was a warm summer's evening, just a little before dark and little did I know that before the darkness would set in, my world would be changed.

I was babysitting three of my grandbabies, while their parents were out for "date night". Two of the children were twin boys about 3 years old. The third was my granddaughter, who was about 4 years older than the boys.

Their Mom and Dad had left me in charge for the day and we had a wonderful time playing in the club house. This was my dream home (as I call them in my real estate business). It was the home with all the things I could not afford while raising the family. It had over four thousand square feet with everything I thought would be my bait for my three children and six grandbabies to enjoy. I had nicknamed it the "flip-flop house" because the living area, kitchen and master bedroom were on the second floor allowing me to enjoy a view of the golf course, while the game room and secondary bedrooms were on the first floor. It had a grand entry with double stairs that welcomed you as you entered. Under the massive stairs was the grandchildren's hidden toy room named the "Club House".

The boys were the age when they were into everything and every corner of the house had now been explored by them and so a little excursion seemed to be a good way to get them calmed down before bedtime. I decided I could entertain them with an old fashion trip to feed the ducks on our golf course. I knew that they always enjoyed a ride on the family golf cart and the pond was much too long of a walk for the little ones, so I thought we all would enjoy this pleasant way to end a perfect day!

I put all three children on the golf cart and added the family dog, Sandy and off we went to find the ducks. The sunset was outstanding as we drove up to the pond. About a dozen ducks were lazily swimming and enjoying the beautiful ambiance. No golfers were left on the course and there were no walkers along the path, only us to enjoy the evening.

Out came the day-old bread and we all jumped off the cart to feed the ducks. We had to walk down the grassy slope to where the ducks were and we all sat down quietly to get them to come up to get their treats. Of course the children loved the experience and I was enjoying watching them try to feed the ducks. We all loved it. The perfect evening.

In a split second, I heard the sound of the golf cart. I anxiously turned around to see if another golf cart was coming to share the evening with us. There was no other cart! One of the twins was sitting on our golf cart and was trying to drive it. I would never have suspected that this could have happened so fast. One moment we were all feeding the ducks and the next, I had a run-away golf cart with one of my precious 3-year-old grandsons at the wheel.

I had not taken the keys out of the starter, thinking I could lose them while playing with the children. All the baby had to do is get on and push the gas pedal and off the cart would go...right into the water! My instant thought was I will just run over and stop it but the cart was moving so fast that in order to save my grandson from going into the water, I got between the cart and water. I had no idea how heavy a golf cart was. They looked so light-weight but what I didn't know was the cart was powered by multiple batteries that weigh a lot and were very powerful. While I was fighting to use all my strength to stop the cart, my grandson was turning the wheel and the cart was now headed toward a wooden bridge.

It all happened so fast and all I was experiencing was my protective grandmother instinct to save my grandson. In a matter of seconds, the golf cart hit the bridge and my left foot was caught between the two.

My foot was smashed and blood was everywhere. I had saved my grandson at the cost of almost losing my foot. Thank goodness my granddaughter was old enough to help me get everyone back on the cart. Except my poor little dog, who was so upset his master was hurt that he ran along the side of cart, as I tried to get us back to civilization to get help.

I had always had a phobia about blood. To my thinking, my life was in the blood and if it came out of my body (even with a small cut), I would faint. This time I couldn't faint; it was vital to hold myself together and get someone to help before I lost consciousness. Thank goodness in crisis, we can do remarkable things and somehow, I made the drive back to a road and saw a house with lights on. I sent my granddaughter for help and they called an ambulance, rescued the children and kept them calm until family help got there.

I was bleeding so badly that as soon as help arrived, I went into shock. The last thing I remember was giving my rescuers my son's cell number, so he could get the children and I was taken off to the hospital. I woke up with nurses and doctors all around me trying to stop the bleeding and save my foot. They did x-rays and told me every bone in my foot had been crushed by the impact and I probably would never walk on it again.

As soon as my son got the children under control and back in their parents' hands, he came to the hospital. Danny was a Bible student and was attending Rhema Bible College under Kenneth Hagin. He immediately started praying prayers of faith and healing to our heavenly Father.

Our feet have more bones than any other part of our body and receiving the news that I would never be the same, was just not acceptable. Danny and I agreed in prayer for a complete healing and while I continually prayed in the Holy Spirit, Danny made a list of Scriptures about healing and bones coming together. One of those Scriptures in Ezekiel 37 :6-7 is where God told Ezekiel, *"I'll attach sinews to you, put meat on your bones, cover you with skin, and breathe life into you...As I prophesied, there was a sound and, oh, rustling! The bones moved and came together, bone to bone."* I fell asleep with the list of Scriptures under my injured foot as I was claiming them. *"And before you know it the God of peace will come down on Satan with both feet, stomping him into the dirt. Enjoy the best of Jesus." Romans 16:20*. What power we have to be able to claim God's Word and see God perform it in our own lives. The words of life and death are in the power of the tongue; I was putting God's Word in action. I put Satan's destructive tactics under my authority through the power of Jesus Christ.

The next day, a second set of x-rays was taken and all the bones were found in their original place again and not one was broken! My skin and muscles still needed mending but I walk today without any pain from that foot. The scars are still a visual reminder of the healing power Jesus provides. God gave us promises for healing of all our sickness and accidents through the Kingdom of God. And I claimed my healing and God was faithful to heal me!

During an innocent moment, my life could have been changed for the worst but God intervened, saved and healed what Satan meant for bad but God used for good. Kingdom life is the reason for the happy ending. Jesus died for our health and prosperity and miracles are for all who claim them in his kingdom. God says, *"Beloved, I wish above all things that thou mayest prosper and be in health, even as thy soul prospereth."* 3 John 1:2 KJ

Satan has tried several other times to take my health, but I stand firm on God's Word. God has healed me every time and saved my life! I enjoy God's promises of health and prosperity in his kingdom.

I tell this story to share just one of my healings. I believe Jesus knew when He went to the cross for forgiveness for our sins, that he would also provide 7 ways we could be healed. Take advantage of everything Jesus provided at Calvary and know all of God's healing power is for you in his kingdom on earth.

Kingdom Thinking

How many ways have you been healed? What were the circumstances around the healing?

What is the estimated amount of time between the creation of man and Jesus' birth? Explain how a day can be as a thousand years?

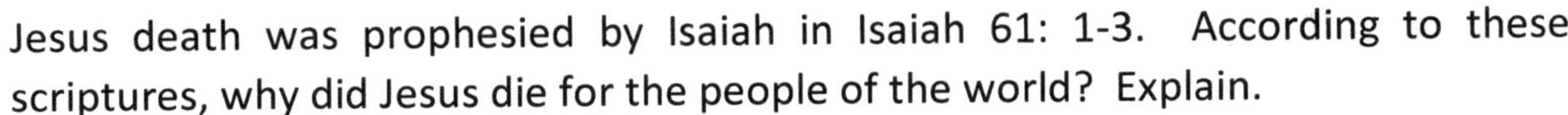

Jesus death was prophesied by Isaiah in Isaiah 61: 1-3. According to these scriptures, why did Jesus die for the people of the world? Explain.

Is it your "joy" that gives you strength? How does forgiveness play into "joy" in your life according to the scriptures?

Some of the most serious hurts are hidden (emotional) injuries that are passed down through bloodlines. When you look at your family, do you see any generational curses that need to be healed so they will not affect future generations?

Keys to the Kingdom

L0CATION	PLACE OF SHEDDING	HEALING REDEEMED	SPOKEN WORDS
Garden of Gethsemane	Sweat blood	Willpower	Father, not my will but your will!
City of Jerusalem, Whipping Post	"39" Lashes Stripes on his back	Health	By his stripes we were healed!
Whipping Post Floor	Crown of thorns on his head	Prosperity	God gives power to get wealth that his covenant may be established!
Crucifixion	Nail–pierced hands	Dominion over ALL on the earth	Everything our hands touch will prosper!
Crucifixion	Nail-pierced feet	Authority over Fear and Terror	Everywhere your foot treads shall be yours!
Crucifixion	Heart pierced	Happiness and Joy	Joy of the Lord is our strength
The Entire Process	Bruised	Inner Hurts and Iniquities	We are a new creature. Old things have passed away and all things have become new.

Merciful Thanks

by Joy E. Miller

Blessed be God, who hath not turned away my prayer of his mercy for me. *Psalms 66:22*
While on vacation walking the Bohemian streets of Paris, I spotted a woman doing her morning grocery shopping. She appeared middle aged, but the years had not been kind to her. Her fragile body was bent double from a large bump on her back; it caused her to use a walking cane for stability. My heart went out to her. I realized how blessed I was for my perfect health, and breathed a prayer for her continued strength.

After an hour of shopping I came upon a lesser cathedral in the shadow of the famous Notre Dame. This was preferred by the locals to avoid the large tourist crowds. To my surprise, there she was—the same little lady—kneeling on the steps, begging for alms and praying for mercy. Mercy for her family. Mercy for herself. All the while blessing God for all He had done for her.

I realized that all over the world, people just like this frail lady, pray to our God and He honors their prayers. God is faithful to hear each prayer, and faithful to show His love and mercy to all, wherever, and from whomever those prayers come from.

The Red Cup in this painting represents the provision and protection that Jesus' blood provides His followers.

CHAPTER 7

Kingdom Helper

How do we stay in his presence and communication with the Father?

Covenant Relationship

God is a covenant God and he has made covenant with those who follow him. Covenant has to be a two-way street. God and you both have to be in agreement for it to be legal.

Our covenant with God:

- Is a binding agreement.
- Is an endless agreement that lasts forever.
- Allows his blessings and purposes for us to be fulfilled.
- Allows us to fully possess all of our inheritance.
- Should not be entered into lightly but sacredly.

In today's society, people freely make commitments and promises that are easily broken. Whether it is a marriage covenant, business contract or a national commitment between nations, God expects his people to honor our words. God does not enter into covenant with us lightly nor does he allow us to think lightly of it. We both must come into agreement for life and with that comes hundreds of promises and blessings.

The first covenant was made with Adam. His covenant included making:

- man in the image of God,
- man fruitful and able to multiply,
- man to subdue the earth, and
- dominion over things of the earth.

Either party can break a covenant. The good thing about God is that he doesn't break his covenant with man, even though man has continually broken his with God. Adam's part of the covenant was to obey God, commune with him and oversee his creation. God's only command to Adam was not to eat from the Tree of Knowledge of Good and Evil and even told them that the moment he did, *"you're dead." Genesis 2:17.* One of the blessings that God gave Adam after the covenant was the creation of a beautiful woman named Eve. Adam was to have dominion over her and I'm sure she knew what God had told Adam, for when the serpent appeared she was able to tell him what God had said. The serpent was beguiling and asked her a trick question;

> *"Do I understand that God told you not to eat from any tree in the garden?"* She answered him, *"Not at all. We can eat from the trees in the garden. It's only about the tree in the middle of the garden that God said, 'Don't eat from it, don't even touch it or you'll die.'"* The sly serpent now told her a lie... *"YOU WON'T DIE. God knows that the moment you eat from the tree, you'll see what's really going on. You'll be just like God, knowing everything, ranging all the way from good to evil..." Genesis 2:17*

God was very serious when he said, *"Don't eat or touch the fruit of the tree or you will die."* In the King James Version of the Bible it quotes Satan; *"Ye shall not surely die."* Satan was trying to put doubt in Eve's mind. After causing the confusion of what God had really said, Satan continued on with the temptation. Eve knew Satan was tempting her but she wanted to have all knowledge, just as God did. She ate the fruit and immediately went to Adam to give it to him, and he ate it too. The Scriptures do not directly tell us if Eve's eyes were opened as soon as she ate, but it does say that after Adam ate, both of their eyes were opened and they knew they were naked.

Adam was the covenant maker with God and he broke the covenant when he dishonored God's command not to eat of the Tree of Knowledge of Good and Evil. This was the first sin. Scholars have different opinions of why he ate of the fruit, but most agree that Eve was his responsibility and that possibly he did not want to lose her as his companion and/or that he knew that she would have knowledge of evil and he would not. Whatever the reason, he knew it was wrong and he ate the fruit which broke the covenant God had made with Adam. He no longer had dominion over all the earth and the composition of the earth changed from that moment on.

It was disobedience that caused the covenant to be broken. At that point, God needed a way to redeem man back to himself. In the Old Testament, God had six different covenants with man; all which were broken and man lost his blessing each time he broke a covenant. Man had proven he could not keep a covenant. But, God had a plan from the beginning of time—"The Covenant" and the "Everlasting Covenant" would be established in the New Testament where God would provide a creative and redemptive way for man to re-establish covenant relationship with himself for eternity.

The New Covenant is for those who have made Jesus Lord of their life and are born again. Through Jesus' blood that was shed, humanity received forgiveness and remission of the penalty of sin by Jesus' death, burial and resurrection. We are justified, righteous and sanctified to the Lord and God has adopted us as sons and daughters. As well, God has many promises in the New Testament for believers. Whoa, that is a study all its own; but, to say the least, man gets a lot for his faith in God's Son, Jesus Christ.

The Everlasting Covenant is also taught in the New Testament. Once we have accepted Jesus as Savior and Lord, we are eligible at the time of Jesus' second coming to be restored to original eternal covenant relationship.

We must remember that any earthly covenant relationship can be broken and that both parties have a responsibility in order to receive the fulfillment of the entire covenant. (An in-depth study is recommend for a complete understanding of God's covenant relationships and its expectations and rewards).

A large part of God's expectation of us when we enter into covenant with him is that as believers, we do not allow any other "god" to be more important than our "God of the Universe".

> *"God spoke all these words: I am GOD, your God, who brought you out of Egypt, out of a life of slavery. No other gods, only me. No carved gods of any size, shape, or form of anything whatever, whether of things that fly or walk or swim. Don't bow down to them and don't serve them because I am God, your GOD, and I'm a jealous God, punishing the children for any sins their parents pass on to the third, and yes, even to the fourth generation of those who hate me."*
>
> *"But I'm unswervingly loyal to the thousands who love me and keep my commandments. Exodus 20:1-6*

This is his first commandment and he takes it seriously. And he re-established it in the New Testament. Jesus said it like this: *"Love the Lord your God, with all your passion and prayer and muscle and intelligence. This is the most important, the first on any list. But there is a second to set alongside it. 'Love others as well as you love yourself.'" Luke 10:27*

To enter into this covenant with God, you should always remember that it cannot be done without you freely deciding you want to have a relationship with God, the Father. The next steps are for you to submit, resist the devil and draw near to God. It will then be easier to walk with God, if you know and understand his Word and let him reveal to you its deeper meaning. It is part of his plan for you to accept that he has a purpose for you and for you to seek your destiny in him. This is the beginning of wisdom; to realize and have faith that God will provide all your needs. As his follower, you will then want to work to achieve and follow his commands each day and be willing to fight the devil and his demons to accomplish what God has told you is yours. This is daily life in the Kingdom of God!

The 3 "P's" – Nuts and Bolts of Prayer, Praise and Presence

Prayer with Faith

What is prayer? A simple question, the answer which fills up hundreds of books. Prayer is simply talking with God! If we go back to Genesis, God didn't make it that complicated. Adam and Eve daily walked with God through the garden, and communicated directly with him. After they sinned, they no longer retained the ability to stay in that same relationship. Because God is holy, he cannot tolerate ungodliness. They now had sin that stood between them and direct communication with God. Through the Old Testament, God set up 6 different covenants with man, which were governed by the Law of Moses, and could have bridged the gap that sin had created. The people proved over and over again that they would continue to sin and only became very religious trying to keep the letter of the law. The law allowed only priests and prophets to pray directly to God. After thousands of years of communicating with God through the men of God, Jesus went to the cross for all God's people, in order to establish a New Covenant which would permanently bridge the gap between God and humanity.

Jesus' blood would cover man's sin. Jesus prophesied this to his disciples at the Lord's Supper the night before his death:

> *"This is my blood, God's new covenant poured out for many people for the forgiveness of sins." Matthew 26:28*

In Hebrews, it explains the importance God put on blood for remission of sins.

> *"But when the Messiah arrived, high priest of the superior things of the new covenant, he bypassed the old tent and it's trappings* **(Old Testament Covenants)** *in this created world and went straight into heaven's 'tent'—the true Holy Place—once and for all. He also bypassed the sacrifices consisting of goat and calf blood, instead using his own blood as the price to set us free once and for all." Hebrews 9:11-12*
>
> *"Like a will that takes effect when someone dies, the covenant was put into action at Jesus' death. His death marked the transition from the old plan* **(Old Testament Covenants)** *cancelling the old obligations and accompanying sin, and summoning the heirs to receive the eternal inheritance that was promised them. He brought together God and his people in this new way.* **(New Covenant)** *Even the first plan required a death to set it in motion. After Moses had read out all terms of the plan* **(Old Testament Covenants)** *of the law—he took the blood of sacrificed animals and, in a solemn ritual, sprinkled the document and the people who were its beneficiaries. And then he attested its validity with the words... "This is the blood of the covenant commanded by God established with you." Practically everything in a will hinges on a death. That's why blood, the evidence of death, is used so much in our tradition, especially regarding forgiveness of sins. That accounts for the prominence of blood and death in all these secondary practices that point to the realities of heaven. It also accounts for why, when the real thing takes place these animal sacrifices aren't needed anymore, having served their purpose. For Christ didn't enter the earthly version of the Holy Place* **(Holy of Holies in the Tabernacle)***; he entered the Place Itself* **(Heaven),** *and offered himself to God as the sacrifice for our sins." Hebrews 9:19-24* **[bold words added for clarification]**

Jesus' blood allowed us to clean up our whole lives, inside and out. In God's spiritual kingdom, Jesus offered himself as a perfect human man (God in the flesh) to free us of our sinful ways and allow us to stand and communicate with our Holy God! Now we have a direct way through Jesus himself, to speak directly to God using Jesus' blood and his name.

Prayer is not a religious activity with no power. It is meant to be effective with power! Throughout the ages, every religion uses some form of prayer or meditation to appease their deity. Humans of all religions expect prayer to work and if it doesn't, the people lose their desire to stay engaged in the communication with a "god" that does not respond to their needs. Our God, Jehovah Jireh, says he watches over his Word to perform it. We always get results with our God if we stay engaged with him. Over the 6 thousand years of recorded history in the Bible, many men questioned their ability to do what God told them to do. Noah, Moses, Jeremiah, Elijah, John the Baptist, and the disciples, are just a few of those who acknowledged that without God's personal guidance, they could not accomplish what they were given to do. Both in the New and Old Testament, men used prayer to get God's help when they needed it. In Jeremiah, the prophet argued with God when he was struggling to do God's will. This was God's response:

> *"Don't say, 'I'm only a boy.' I'll tell you where to go and you'll go there. I'll tell you what to say and you'll say it. Don't be afraid of a soul. I'll be right there, looking after you. God's Decree. God reached out, touched his mouth, and said, Look! I've just put my words in your mouth—hand delivered.' And God said, "I'll make every word I give you come true....I'll back you up every inch of the way." Jeremiah 1:7-9, 12, 19.*

And if you read Jeremiah's story, you will find God did back him up each time he needed it. And God will answer our prayers the same way.

Prayers that bring results must be based on God's Word. The Word of God is alive and full of power;

> *"God means what he says. What he says goes. His powerful Word is sharp, as a surgeon's scalpel, cutting through everything, whether doubt of defense, laying us open to listen and obey. Nothing and no one is*

> *impervious to God's Word. We can't get away from it—no matter what." Hebrew 4:12-13*

The Amplified Bible says it this way: that whatever God speaks is *"alive and full of power - making it active, operative, energizing and effective...penetrating to the dividing line of breath of life, soul and spirit, and the joints and marrow (that is, of the deepest parts of our nature) exposing and sifting and analyzing and judging the very thoughts and purposes of the heart."*

God's Word is powerful and active but his Word also gives us rest when we use it in prayers of faith. It might seem odd to say that too much religion is bad... but Paul, the Apostle, explains that it can be. In his letter to the Hebrew church, he shows that we try to do "more versus less", to prove our faithfulness. This would be defined as a religion of works. God's simplistic plan was revealed through Jesus' life of obedience to "his Father's will". This kind of obedience always requires us to live by the acts of faith not works.

We cannot please God without faith! SO.....How then does God define "FAITH"?

> *"The fundamental fact of existence is that this trust in God, this faith, is the firm foundation under everything that makes life worth living. It's our handle of what we can't see." Message Bible*
>
> AND
>
> *"Now faith is the substance of things hoped for, the evidence of things not seen." King James*

You put these two translations of Hebrews 11:1 together and you have a great definition. We can now unpack the spiritual meaning of "FAITH".

Faith is:

- A fundamental act of existence in the spiritual realm.
- Trusting God for everything we need.
- Our foundation of a life worth living.
- Our handle to hold on to in every situation.
- The substance of our hopes and desires.
- The evidence of what cannot be seen or touched!

Prayer is fellowship with God the Father which allows us to be in constant communication with him. He desires us to share our needs and our wants with him through prayer and to utilize our faith, so he can provide for us. In fact, his Word says,

> *"For the eyes of the Lord are over the righteous, and his ears are open unto their prayers..." 1 Peter 3:12 KJ*

Jesus explained his Father's intention when he said, *"Ask and you shall receive, seek and you will find and knock and it shall be opened to you."* (Matthew 7:7-11). God wants to give to us, too. He even says as humans, if our child asks for food, do we want to give him a stone? No, we want to give our children what they want and/or need. Our Father, which is in heaven wants to give good things to those who ask.

> *"Don't bargain with God. Be direct. Ask for what you need. This isn't a cat-and-mouse, hide-and-seek game we're in. If your child asks for bread, do you trick him with sawdust? If he asks for fish, do you scare him with a live snake on his plate? As bad as you are, you wouldn't think of such a thing. You're at least decent to your own children. So don't you think the God who conceived you in love will be even better?" Matthew 7:7-11*

James 4:2 asks a question for you to consider. *"You just wouldn't think of just asking God for it, would you?* Sometimes we don't even think that God cares what we are going through or what we need, so we just don't go to him; but he does care and he says, if we will just ask in his "will", he will be glad to give it to us. Jesus said *"Ask in my name, according to my will, and he'll most certainly give it to you. Your joy will be a river overflowing its banks." John 16:24*

When the disciples asked Jesus to teach them how to pray, he used four verses to give us an example, we call it "The Lord's Prayer"! It has so much in it; that it is a study all its own. Stop and read it now and pray that God will quicken it, in depth to you. (The bold words are the King James Version that most of us have memorized. The *italicized* words are the Message Bible Translation)

The Lord's Prayer

Our Father, which art in heaven, Hallowed be thy name.

Our Father in heaven, Reveal who you are.

Thy kingdom come.

Set the world right;

Thy will be done, as in heaven, so in earth.

Do what's best--as above, below.

Give us day by day our daily bread.

Keep us alive with three square meals.

And forgive us our sins

And forgive us our debt, as we forgive our debtors.

Keep us forgiven with you and forgiving others.

And lead us not into temptation;

But deliver us from evil;

Keep us safe from ourselves and the Devil.

For Thine is the kingdom, and the power, and the glory

You're in charge! You can do anything you want!

You're ablaze in beauty!

Forever. Amen

Yes, Yes, Yes

Matthew 6:9-13

Notice it does not say, whatever you want, you can have. Our request needs to be in "God's will". That takes the human wants and desires out of it! The things that would lead us in the opposite direction from God's plan for us would be gone. Those things that allow us to get into trouble would not happen. If we choose our own will, God will allow us to direct our lives and to get any bad results from those decisions. In our world today, we have been taught that we can be whatever we want to be if we are willing to work hard to get it. We are taught it is ok to do whatever makes us feel good! We think we are number one and it doesn't matter what others want; if we want it, go for it! Many of today's churches have even taught that we can pray for anything and if we believe it enough and have faith enough, we will get it! None of this is God's way and none of it will be blessed. Many times we get what we ask for but watch out; we will reap the rewards of a selfish sinful person, if we are asking out of God's will for our own selfish reasons.

I speak at women's conferences and tell my own testimony of learning this lesson. This is a passage from my story "Crossing Over".

"Lesson # 1—Divorce is devastating! And single-parenting is the hardest job on the planet. Lesson # 2—Seeking self-fulfillments can derail you if you are doing it for all the wrong reasons."

I had allowed life to take me down a road of self-pleasures and not made quality decisions at the points of "crossing's overs". I never asked anyone for help. I never asked God whether it was his will or not to do anything. Therefore, I had to face the consequences of those decisions and my chosen path led to some very hard times in my life. I learned my lessons the hard way, but I'm smarter now and I strive to be in God's will.

Jesus only did his Father's will. He told his disciples that he did only what he saw his Father do. How did he see what God the Father was doing in heaven while he was here on earth? Because, Jesus continually lived in the presence of God. He stayed in communication with his Father. Jesus explained himself at length.

> *"I'm telling you this straight. The Son can't independently do a thing, only what he sees the Father doing. What the Father does, the Son does. The Father loves the Son and includes him in everything he is doing." John 5:19-20*

A few chapters later, Jesus told us *"The person who trusts me will not only do what I'm doing but even greater things, because I, on my way to the Father, am giving you the same work to do that I've been doing. You can count on it." John 14:1.* So if Jesus can see what the Father was doing while he was on earth, so can we. We must strive to maintain right relationship and communication with the Father by praying without ceasing, remaining in continual praise and worship, which will lead us into his presence. That is how we stay in God's will!

Jesus said he would give us "keys" to the Kingdom of God.

> *"...You will have complete and free access to God's kingdom, Keys to open any and every door: no more barriers between heaven and earth, earth and heaven. A yes on earth is yes in heaven. A no on earth is no in heaven." Matthew 16:18*

These things are our "Keys" in this Scripture. Would it be better if:

- We have access to HEAVEN to control what happens on EARTH.
- We take OWNERSHIP of our spiritual responsibilities in order to get AUTHORITY to make a real difference in our life.
- We would have FREEDOM and PROVISION because we ask it in the RIGHT WAY.

If prayer works and we get good results, we will continue to use it to communicate and have relationship with our Father God in heaven.

Kenneth E. Hagin, who many claim is the "father of faith for the modern church", explained Matthew 16:18: "The key actually does the unlocking. When we start the car, a key really does the work. A key starts the ignition. But when Jesus gave us the key to do it, Jesus is the key to doing it."

Many times we pray traditionally or ritually, and do not get the results we need. If we use the wrong key (principles), it will not work. However, if we use our faith, his Word and God's will, we will see results and we will see his power at work in our lives.

Prayer is a key to prosperous life in the Kingdom of God. With simple prayer, we can change our future, one prayer at a time, as we have relationship and communication with God.

Praise & Worship leads to His Presence

God is very clear that he loves us to praise him and be thankful for all he has done for us. David, one of God's most devoted followers and worshipers said that *"God inhabits the praises of His people"*. God is looking for people to worship him and if we will only pray, praise and worship him, he will find us. This is God's desire, for God to inhabit us and for us to live in his presence.

Praise and worship can be done many ways. As we start the Lord's Prayer, our first sentence is one of worship, *"our Father who art in heaven, hallowed be thy name."* We should always address him with our thanks for all he has done for us. He loves for us to be specific about the blessings He provides us. Aren't we like that too? Don't we like others to say how much they appreciate things we do for them? God is the same way. There are many valid and beneficial forms and ways to show God how much we love, appreciate and desire to worship him. Whether you are silent or loud or if you are reflective or expressive in your praise and worship...the important thing is to be submitted to God's will; following the Holy Spirit's leadings and seeking him with your whole heart. Many people are very familiar with less exuberant ways of worship, rather than David's way of dancing with all his heart. God loves it all, whether we are bold and exuberant or refined with a bowed head and a formal reverent prayer. He wants us to worship him creatively without being inhibited by traditions. He just appreciates when we honor him with praises. Once we have given him praise, don't you think he would be more receptive to our petitions?

God has given us so many reasons to praise him. Things like enjoying nature encourages us to praise him. We should realize that without God's creation, all this natural beauty in the world would not be on earth for us to enjoy. He loves us to use our five senses: see, taste, hear, smell and feel his creation, so we can appreciate even the small things He created. Enjoying a beautiful sunset, a hummingbird harvesting nectar on a gorgeous flower, or diving to see his beautiful world under the water, smelling the freshness of rain after a shower or touching a newborn baby's soft skin are just a few ways that God takes our breath away by the beauty he has provided for us. We could go on and on about the natural beauty that screams out. Who but our God could have created such a beautiful place for us to worship and praise him!

As a mother, I remember how overcome with praise and worship I was when I held each of my babies and grandchildren in my arms the first time. God even fills us with his love, so as parents we can instantly give love to his new creations.

The mathematics that holds the universe in place, which formulates the air we breathe, causes the rotation of the stars and the planets. His healing power that gives health to a sick child after we prayed for healing; the emotion of happiness when seeing a loved one after years of separation. We have so much to praise him for; and we haven't even touched on the spiritual provisions he has provided, such as forgiveness of sin, eternal life with him and his absolute undeserved LOVE he has for us.

Music leads us into praise and into God's presence for worship. There is nothing like going to church and enjoying the music, with the choir, musical instruments and song leader. Our hardened hearts can be melted, our busy minds can be calmed and our spirits can be lifted to new levels when we sit under a masterful psalmist who creates a heavenly atmosphere that leads us into praise and worship.

Praise should be like breathing, sleeping or eating - just a natural part of our daily living. Not like a habit but a continual appreciation for everything he provides. We should never take anything he does for us for granted.

God takes praise and worship seriously. In the Old Testament, He said,

> *"If any of these survivors fail to make the annual pilgrimage to Jerusalem to worship the King, God-of-the-Angel-Armies, there will be no rain." Zechariah 14:17.*

When you realize that things are conditional, based upon our obedience to God, you will learn to adjust your responses to his request. God told the Israelites to march around Jericho seven times and then shout with praise! When they obeyed, the walls fell down and the Israelites won the battle. You cannot always see what God is doing when you praise and worship him...but you must trust that he is doing something that will change the atmosphere to get the needed results. Many times it takes praise and worship to keep our eyes off the problem and put them on our God who is always working on our behalf. So, praise and worship is our way of utilizing the FAITH that God says we must have to please him.

When we are praising and worshiping, we are expressing his superiority over our inferiority. Let's admit it - God is better and bigger than we are and is able to meet our every need. He is truly awesome and being in his presence inspires us to be in awe of him even more. Now why would God tell the people that if they didn't go to Jerusalem to worship, there would be no rain? The circumstances required it. The Israelites had left Egypt and were to possess their Promise Land, Canaan, which would be a land of milk and honey with luscious fruits and bountiful harvest of grains, which would require "drinks from the rain of heaven" to produce the promises.

> *"Your obedience will give you a long life on the soil that God promised to give your ancestors and their children, a land flowing with milk and honey.*
>
> *The land you are entering to take up ownership isn't like Egypt, the land you left, where you had to plant your own seed and water it yourselves as in a vegetable garden. But the land you are about to cross the river and take for your own is a land of mountains and valleys, it drinks water that rains from the sky. It's a land that God, your God, personally tends—he's the gardener—he alone keeps his eye on it all year long.*
>
> *From now on if you listen obediently to the commandments that I am commanding you today, love God, your God, and serve him with everything you have with you, He'll take charge of sending the rain at the right time, both autumn and spring rains, so that you'll be able to harvest your grain, your grapes, your olives. He'll make sure there's plenty of grass for your animals. You'll have plenty to eat." Deuteronomy 11:9-15*

By honoring God, we are saying that he is sovereign; that he will bring the rain that is needed for our prosperity and that there is not any other source but him to provide it!

Another way you can praise and worship is by humbling yourself before him.

> *"and my people, my God-defined people, respond by humbling themselves, praying, seeking my presence, and turning their backs on their wicked lives.*

I'll be there ready for you. I'll listen from heaven, forgive their sins, and restore their land to health." 2 Chronicle 7:14

The word humble is "kama", a Hebrew word for "worship". It means to bend the knee, representing to humiliate, bring down low, into subjection, humble, subdue. Just as we raise our hands in praise and submission, we can humble ourselves by kneeling to our God in his presence. Some of God's most powerful answers to our prayers happen when we humble ourselves by getting on our knees or by lying prostate on the floor before him, worshiping and seeking him for our answers.

Let's define praise and worship:

- PRAISE is more of a jubilant activity, with actions of singing, dancing, and shouting in appreciation of his actions or in faith to his future responses!
- WORSHIP is the ability to look at God from a humble, lowered or bowed head in reverence to an awesome God...when we are not dependent on his response but just for who he is.

How does God define what a true worshiper is? When Jesus met the woman of Samaria and talked with her about worshiping, he explains the old form of worship in the Old Testament and the new form of worship which would be performed after his death and resurrection. He explained it like this:

"Our ancestors worshiped God at this mountain, but you Jews insist that Jerusalem is the only place of worship. Believe me, woman, the time is coming when you Samaritans will worship the Father neither here at this mountain nor there in Jerusalem. You worship guessing in the dark, we Jews worship in the clear light of day...But the time is coming—it has, in fact, come—when what you're called will not matter and where you go to worship will not matter."

"IT'S WHO YOU ARE AND THE WAY YOU LIVE THAT COUNT BEFORE GOD. You must engage your Spirit in the pursuit of Truth. THAT'S THE KIND OF PEOPLE THE FATHER IS OUT LOOKING FOR; those who are simply and honestly themselves before him, in their worship. God is sheer being itself—Spirit. Those who worship him must do it out of their very being, their

> *spirits, their true selves, in adoration."* *John 4:20-24 (Caps and underlining for importance.)*

It's not where you worship; no mountain, no city or no church will make you a true worshiper. It has nothing to do with whether you are a man or woman, Jew or Gentile, Baptist or Assembly of God. It doesn't matter if you worship morning or night, feast or holiday, winter or summer. God is looking for you to worship him in Spirit; the place where we have true knowledge and understanding of who God is and with a heart that is humble and striving for holiness. These are the worshippers: those that seek God. Jesus explained it like this: *"Love the Lord your God with all your passion and prayer and intelligence." Matthew 22:37*

God excels and benefits when the atmosphere is saturated by worship and praise. He even gets excited and wants to meet and exceed your expectations of him. When Paul and Silas were beaten and thrown in jail, they began to sing praises in their darkest hours of humiliation and pain. They sang until God sent his glory down in the form of an earthquake that shook the jail until the doors broke open and their chains broke off. I bet they never thought that would happen, but God loved what he heard. He knew it was adoration from Paul and Silas for who God was and why they loved him in spite of their pain and so he surprised them with their freedom. Praise and worship changed the atmosphere; "rain" came and protection and provision followed. Our greatest test can be the best time to praise and worship so God can enter the scene with greater provision than we ever dreamed or hoped for.

As you worship, you are sacrificing your life on an altar of surrender as a living sacrifice. God in return will exceed your expectation with his own surpassing abundance for you!

> *"God can do anything, you know—far more than you could ever imagine or guess or request in your wildest dreams! He does it not by pushing us around but by working within us, his Spirit deeply and gently within us.*
>
> *Glory to God in the church!*
>
> *Glory to God in the Messiah, in Jesus!*
>
> *Glory down all the generations!*

Glory through all millennia! Oh Yes!" Ephesian 3:20-21

Prayer, Praise and Worship bring us into God's Presence.

The 3 "P's" – nuts and bolts are not meant to be used as occasional spiritual rituals when things get hard or tough. They are not to be tools of impulse or emotion. They are to be keys of daily living in the kingdom. Their purpose is to bring us to the highest and best place in God...his PRESENCE! It is in his presence that God can do his greatest miracles and show his gracious and loving nature. We have to cultivate his presence in our lives in order to please God. It is the lifestyle of the Kingdom of God! These keys make up the culture of his kingdom!

Some people believe that you should pray and worship in silence. They stand in church and listen in silence while the pastor says a prayer, reverently sing a few psalms and worship God in silence. Our God is alive and well and loves his people to respond to him with all of their might, strength and emotions. He speaks to us and says that his people will know his voice and he wants to hear our voice. God asks us to shout, dance and be jubilant in our praise and worship. Here is how John the disciple, describes heaven in his vision.

> *"I looked again. I heard a company of Angels around the Throne, the Animals, and the Elders—ten thousand times ten thousands their number, thousand after thousands after thousand, in full song:*
>
> > *The slain Lamb is worthy!*
> >
> > *Take the power, the wealth, the wisdom, the strength!*
> >
> > *Take the honor, the glory, the blessing!*
>
> *Saying with a loud voice, worthy is the Lamb that was slain to receive power, and riches, and wisdom, and strength, and honor, and glory, and blessing. Then I heard every creature in heaven and earth, in underworld and sea, join in, all voices in all places singing:*
>
> > *To the One on the Throne! To the Lamb!*
> >
> > *The blessing, the honor, the glory, the strength,*
> >
> > *For age after age after age,*

The four animals called out, 'OH, Yes!' The Elders fell to their knees and worshiped" *Revelation 5:11*

This is just one of the many examples of what worshiping in "Spirit and Truth" would look like. Let's look at one more example of outrageous worship that completely abandoned human inhibitions. King David loved to praise God and worshiped him from the time he was a young shepherd boy, when God chose him as the future King of Israel, until his death. He is the known author of most of the Psalms, primarily actual songs that he sang in his personal and public service to God. These songs tell his amazing journeys of serving God. David always gave God the glory for all of his conquests while building Israel, part of God's earthly kingdom.

In 2 Samuel 6 is the story of David's conquest to bring the "Ark of Covenant" back to his headquarters. The Ark was the place where God's presence resided until Solomon, David's son, would build God's temple in Jerusalem. When David and his soldiers recovered the Ark, David felt the presence of God would cause him to prosper and to confirm to the region that he was the anointed, and would legalize his kingship and exalt his kingdom to world prominence.

When he arrived with the Ark, David led his soldiers into the city with praise and gratitude for the treasures of war. They all praised God with all their might even to abandonment of all physical and mental embarrassments. Michal, one of David's wives, demanded that he not be such a disgrace to the people; but David continued on with the whole country to leap in dance, to shout with praise, for the things God had done for them. His praise turned to worship with burnt and peace offerings. God was pleased with the celebration and David became a conquering king and built the nation of Israel through many battles. He continually depended on God to guide him through each battle to success! Because Michal refused to praise and worship and despised David for exalting God, she remained barren and would have no child for the remainder of her life. David's last recorded words to Michal were, *"In God's presence I'll dance all I want!...I'll dance to God's glory...I'll gladly look like a fool!" 2 Samuel 6:21-23.*God wants us to desire his presence that much; to recklessly involve ourselves in prayer, praise and worship for the purpose of honoring him by being in his presence. Are you willing to exalt God over yourself and forget the silent prayers and expose your love for him in any way God requests? As for me, I want all God has for me and I am willing to give all of myself as a living sacrifice to my God! Are YOU willing?

Kingdom Thinking

Name the first covenant. Who were the parties and what were God's 4 provisions for Man?

How do you define "covenant"? Have you entered into covenant with God? If so when and where? What is your salvation testimony?

Name 3 earthly covenant relationships you have entered into. What were the covenant provisions?

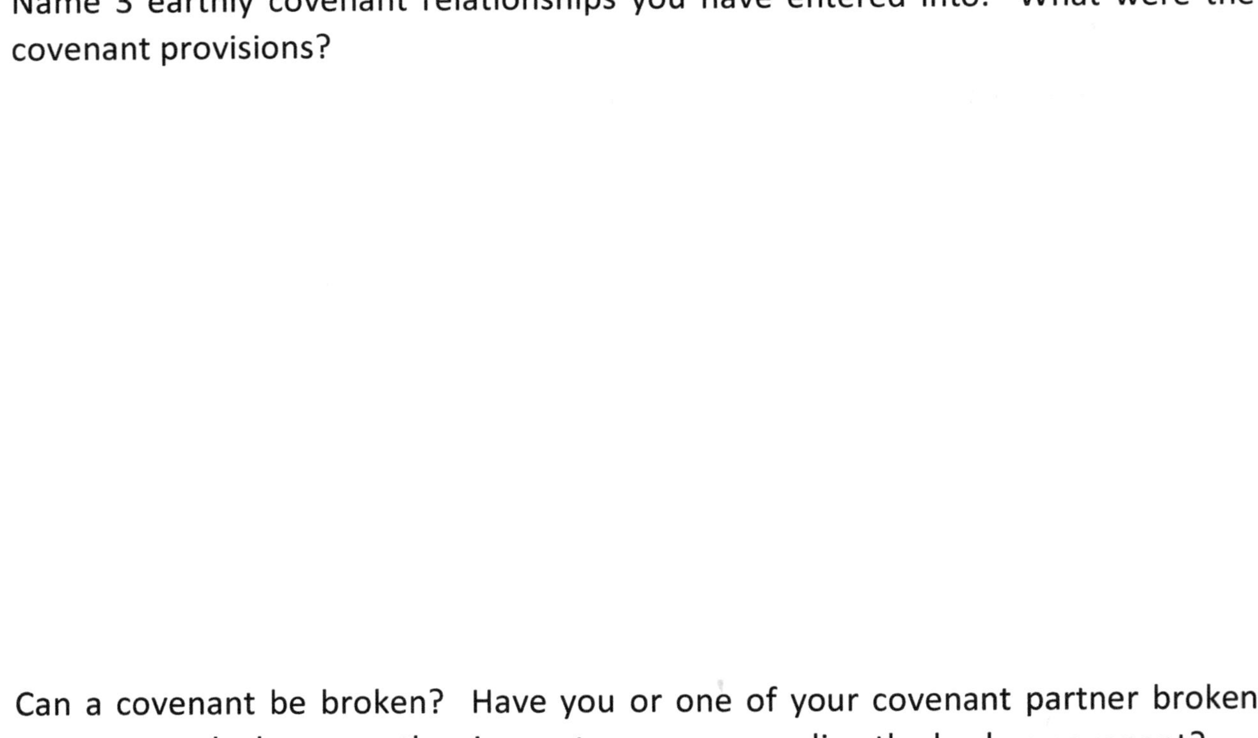

Can a covenant be broken? Have you or one of your covenant partner broken covenant and what were the circumstances surrounding the broken covenant?

Do you believe God is angry with you when covenant is broken? How can it be repaired?

Was Eve a covenant partner? How? Who sinned, Adam or Eve? Why?

Name three prayer keys to the Kingdom of God.

Name four ways to practice praise and worship. What is your favorite way to worship God?

What is the importance of “rain” in reference to worship or being in God’s Presence?

Explain worship and praise in Spirit and Truth?

Keys to the Kingdom: Covenant

- It takes both God and us to enter into covenant relationship.
- God does not break his covenants. Man has broken all the covenants before The New Covenant was made with Jesus.
- When Adam ate from the tree, the first covenant was broken.
- Eve and all future generations lost this covenant because of sin.
- The New Covenant was for all who believe Jesus is their Savior.
- The success steps for the New Covenant are to submit, resist the devil and draw near to God.
- The Everlasting Covenant will begin when Jesus returns to earth for his Church.
- Love the Lord your God, with all your passion and prayer and intelligence. Love others as well as you love yourself.

Keys to the Kingdom: Prayer

- Prayer is not a religious activity with no power. It is meant to be effective with power!
- Prayers that bring results must be based on God's Word.
- We cannot please God without faith!
- Prayer is fellowship with the Father. Ask and you shall receive, seek and you will find and knock and it shall be opened to you.
- Our request needs to be in "God's will".
- You will have complete and free access to God's kingdom.

Keys to the Kingdom: Presence

- God is very clear that he loves us to praise him and be thankful for all he has done for us.
- We should always address him in prayer with our thanks for all he has done for us.
- Music leads us into praise and into God's presence for worship.

- When we are praising and worshiping, we are expressing his superiority over our inferiority.
- PRAISE is more of a jubilant activity.
- WORSHIP is the ability to look at God from a humble, lowered or bowed head in reverence to an awesome God.
- Love the Lord your God with all your passion and abandon all human reasoning.
- God excels and benefits when the atmosphere is saturated by worship and praise.
- God always shows up when we honor him in the "3 P's" of prayer, praise and worship, which leads to his presence.

CHAPTER 8

Kingdom Time

Restore and Recover

The Bible is full of stories of restoration. Our God is a powerful God of redeeming and restoring. Satan, the enemy, attempts to steal and destroy what God means for good. But God has a plan to recover it all!

If Jesus' ministry had a theme, it would be restoring mankind to God's perfect order. Let's look at a sampling of miracles of recovery while Jesus was on earth.

- Jesus restored health to the sick.
- He restored sight to the blind.
- He restored lost limbs to the lame.
- He restored the lepers to society.
- He restored freedom to the demon possessed.
- He raised the dead to life.
- He restored the emotionally wounded.
- Jesus raised himself to life after being dead for 3 days.
- He restored sinners to God.
- And after he ascended into heaven, the restoring power of the Holy Spirit was given to all his followers.

Since Jesus' crucifixion, millions and millions of people have been restored to eternal life and relationship with God, because of what Jesus did for us. Peter, one of the disciples of Jesus, said that Christ's work was a work of grace that would restore, confirm, strengthen and establish us. I completely agree.

As Christians, we should always be seeking and searching for restoration in our personal and spiritual life. The early days of the Church's restoration after Jesus' death was a time of sadness and darkness from the truths that Jesus had taught. The "Middle Ages" began and continued through the 1500's. When the disciples and other believers of the first century church died, there were only the scribes' written accounts of the times. The stories and the Scriptures of the New Testament joined the ancient scrolls of the Old Testament by transcribing them to new parchment and animal skin scrolls, which were placed in dark caves for their preservation.

None of them were easily accessible to the everyday person for studying. The scribes would make all copies by physically handwriting each scripture individually, so few copies were ever made. There was no physical way for mass distribution of Scriptures until the printing press was invented many years later. So it was only by storytelling, one person to another, that the average person knew anything about the early days of the church. During the Protestant Reformation of the 16th and 17th century, the church's priests and pastors, who could read the Hebrew and Greek language where allowed to read and teach the principles that Jesus introduced. Later the Scriptures were transcribed into Latin which allowed more people access to learn of the early days of the church. The priests and scholars of that time would then pass on the stories along with their own interpretation of them to the common people. The churches only encouraged priests to explore the deeper meanings; therefore, it not only kept the people ignorant but made the churches of that day the gatekeepers of spiritual knowledge. The people accepted whatever the church taught them. This led to commoners having no personal relationship with God; therefore, the church used their knowledge to financially exploit and control the people.

With the Reformation, Martin Luther translated God's Word into the ordinary German language and King James commissioned a translation into English. The rest of Europe followed and with the invention of the printing press, allowing all educated people to read the Bible for themselves. This occurred as recently as 400 years ago. With copies of the Scripture printed for all to study, most of the organized church lost the ability to stop individuals from learning its great truths, except for the uneducated which still remained dependent on the organized churches like the Catholic organization. As more and more people have become highly educated, the Bible has become widely read by all who desired to learn, explore and study the truths that God had prepared for them from the beginning of creation more than 6,000 years ago. This was one of God's greatest restorations - his Word to all people. The body of the Church could then develop and mature to the fullness of its truths:

- The truth of righteousness by faith not works.
- The truth that all Christians were Kings and Priests and the church didn't need to be ruled by corrupt clergymen.
- The truth that baptism was meant for all that believed, rather than new-born babies only.
- The truth that Jesus' blood was shed for remission of sins instead of by confession to the priest or by animal sacrifice.
- The truth that God provided his Holy Spirit to teach and direct Jesus' followers...Etc...Etc...Etc.

These were not new doctrines, but ancient truths that could now be interpreted by other creative individuals who would lead new religious groups to be established. However, all people had the privilege to study, grow and benefit from God's Biblical truths. These truths led to re-discovery of God's covenant to the Jewish people and the nation of Israel, restoration of gifts of the Spirit through the Charismatic movement, the establishment of the five-fold ministry as taught by the apostles, and great commission for the soul-winning movements all over the world during the 19th, 20th and 21st century. God is not finished restoring his church yet. For about 1500 years, much of what Jesus taught was kept a secret but in the last 400 years great progress has been made, and new truths that have been hidden in the Scriptures are continually being revealed.

The complete restoration process will continue until Jesus returns to earth for his church at the time of the "rapture" told about in Revelation, the last book in the Bible.

Call to the Kingdom Today: **Jesus is saying to his Believers by his Spirit:**

"TIME is SHORT;

My PEOPLE are NOT Ready;

TELL Them I'm COMING!"

How do we get ready? Time is short and the signs of our time are constantly before us, reminding us that we need to get ready for Jesus' return, known as the "rapture". Our time on earth is for a purpose and we must take the time we have to get ready for Jesus' return. In order to be ready, we must discover what our destiny is. We are not here just to hold a place in time until he returns, but to prepare the way for his return. We must be effective in the use of time we have here on earth, to get our assignment completed. And we must use the Kingdom of God principles to get it accomplished.

Ephesians 5 tells how God expects us to live effectively and successfully in his kingdom. *"Watch what God does, and then you do it, like children who learn proper behavior from their parents." Ephesians 5:1.* This was Jesus' way of living life. He said he only did what he saw his Father do. Everything could be summed up with that, but God knows we want more detailed instructions; so Paul, the apostle and writer of Ephesians, continues on with the following instructions for Christians to live by:

- *Mostly what God does is love you. Keep company with him and learn a life of love.*
- *His love was not cautious but extravagant and we should love him the same way.* (This is one of your 10 Commandants – To love the Lord your God with all your heart, mind and soul.)
- *Don't allow love to turn into lust.*
- *Don't use people or religion just for what you can get out of them.* (Strong emphasis is placed on this with a conclusion that doing this will get you nowhere near the Kingdom of God.)
- *Don't let yourselves get taken in by religious smooth talk.* (It says that this brings on the wrath of God for this disobedience.)
- *Follow the bright light of Jesus which will make your life way plain.*
- *Figure out what will please Christ, and then do it.*
- *Don't waste your time on unfruitful works of evil.*
- *Wake up out of death and walk in the light God provides. Be smart in all you do.*
- *Redeem the time and use time wisely.*
- *Understand the will of God for your time is short.*
- *Live full in the Spirit of God.*

All of these are important to God. We must learn to love as God does. Without that, how can we win others over to our God? We are his representatives and he instructs us to live life loving others and let others see God's love in us. Part of our kingdom walk is to be smart and godly in all we do, so others will notice our abundant life. Paul also tells us to "see that we walk circumspectly" or cautiously to what he is telling us to do. So we should take this list seriously.

The last three things on this list are what I want to concentrate on for this study. They will help us to get ready and be prepared for Jesus' return to his earthly kingdom.

Key 1 – Redeem the time and use time wisely.

This is not earthly time management principles, but supernatural time management principles. We need a revelation and activation of what we need to do, to use kingdom time wisely.

To redeem something is to buy back or exchange for a better value. We are to manage time wisely and to have kingdom purpose with the time we have. God created time very purposely and he says our days on earth are numbered and we should not waste any time. Throughout the Bible, God was also faced with redeeming his time. He did this by stopping time, suspending time, reversing time and accelerating time for his purposes. All of these would be considered supernatural. It is for sure, we as humans cannot stop, suspend, reverse or accelerate time. Time exists and is constant for us on earth. Time has 60 seconds to a minute, 60 minutes to an hour, twenty-four hours in a day, etc.

This is part of kingdom living; learning when it's necessary to supernaturally use time as a tool for kingdom purposes. This allows us to put time to work for us.

Key 2 - Understand the "will of God" because your time is short.

> *"Good friend, don't forget all I've taught you; take to heart my commands. They'll help you live a long, long time, a long life lived full and well." Proverbs 3:1-2* In the King James Bible, it says it this way: *"For length of days, and long life, and peace, shall be added to thee."*

So through obedience to his commands, we can have time and peace added to us. If God spoke to you that he wanted you to get up each morning to spend time with him, wouldn't it be worth it to get up earlier each morning and give God your first fruits in order to have time stretched for you? Quality of life, many times is when we are able to get our work done in a timely manner so we can have extra time at the end of the day to enjoy the gifts God has given us. It is not only in number of days added at the end of our life but it is supernatural time lengthening each day, so we can enjoy kingdom life.

Time was one of God's first creations. *"God spoke: 'Light!' And light appeared. God saw light was good and separated light from dark. God named the light Day, he named the dark Night. It was evening, it was morning—Day One." Genesis 1:2-5.* God used the separation of light and dark to make time with days and nights, and then divided time into the months, years and seasons. After God created the earth, heavens, animals and man, then he gave man authority over God's handcrafted world which includes dominion and authority over time! In the first book in the New Testament, Matthew, Jesus told the disciples, "all power is given unto me in heaven and in earth." And then Jesus commissioned the disciples to go out and do the works that he did and greater! Time if used unwisely is wasted, not doing things God has assigned for us to do.

Key 3 - Live full in the Spirit of God.

We are his disciples, so God gave us the same authority over time as he gave Jesus. If we can grasp this truth, we truly can be living the kingdom life here on earth. We must live as Jesus lived through a spirit-filled life.

As humans, we think time is limited, but in the spirit, time has no limits. If we are in the spirit, we have as much time as needed to do God's purposes. We need to change our thinking about time, and then we could change our faith; to perform the same kind of miracles as Jesus did here on the earth.

Examples of "Time Miracles"

Most of the miracles of the Bible could be related to "time miracles". In Joshua 10:12-13, it states that Joshua spoke to God saying *"Stop, Sun, over Gibeon; Halt, Moon over the Aijalon Valley."* God honored those words of faith and the battle was fought that very day until all the enemies of Israel were defeated, then God allowed the sun to go down over the valley. Time stopped; the sun stopped moving (causing time to stop) and the moon stood still. Joshua understood his authority and used it, to benefit the people of God. Time stood still! Through the authority of God, through his Son Jesus, we have that same authority.

God tells us that it is our responsibility to redeem time. It is one of the principles of the Kingdom of God. We can redeem time by reversal, suspension, lengthening, stretching or acceleration. As Christians, we need to understand that time is a gift and to use it wisely. If we can gain revelation of what God meant by "redeem the time", then we could ask him to show us how, when and where, to use the time miracle process. With godly revelation and studying the miracles that Jesus did, we discover that many of those miracles were miracles using "time redemption". Understanding this will build your faith and encourage you in the fact: if Jesus used time redemption principles, then we can too. Jesus said we can do the same miracles that he did and even greater. Then, this type of miracle (time redemption) is accessible to us today. These time miracles are not just a fictional story in a science fiction novel. When we begin to walk in God's revelation of miracles, we will grow and experience more of his glory in our lives and we will be propelled to walk in his wisdom of kingdom principles. God's revelation takes us higher and opens our minds to deeper truths. It will cause us to want to know God better and go to new places "in the spirit" with him, and help us display his glory here, on the earth. This is how we spiritually grow and bear fruit for him.

We desire to do miracles like Jesus did; but we limit our abilities because we do not understand that miracles are a manipulation of time. We don't need to understand every step of the process in order to walk in the supernatural miracles of God. In fact, if you wait for understanding, you will never walk in them. You must walk in FAITH to perform MIRACLES, so the blind can see and the deaf can hear and thousands of unbelievers will accept Jesus as their Lord and Savior in the last days before the rapture.

Let's look at things we have accepted as miracles but never considered them as a manipulation of time. God led the Israelites into the desert for 40 years and their shoes and clothes never wore out. Did they stop in one place, take their shoes off and camp for 40 years? No, they continually walked in the harsh conditions of the Sinai Desert yet, their shoes and clothes didn't wear out! How? God stopped the normal deterioration of their clothing for over a million people. That entire experience of 40 years in the desert was one miracle after another. God moved food from heaven to earth, moved water through rocks, and even divided the Red Sea, so the people could travel on dry land. All this was accomplished by manipulation of time—by stopping or accelerating time. Another example was Moses physical body reacted like a young man's after the 40 years in the desert. The Bible describes him like this: *"Moses was 120 years old when he died. His eyesight was sharp; he still walked with a spring in his step." Deuteronomy 3:4-7* This was a time miracle--suspension or reversal of time!

When Jesus healed people with missing or withered limbs, it was an acceleration of time for growth of new body parts. When he healed the lepers...it could have been a time reversal back to a time of health or an acceleration of time to renewed health. The miracle of a blind man that had no eye, tells of Jesus reaching down and collecting dirt, spitting on it, placing the dirt in the eye socket, in order for a new eye to be formed. Molecules were changed and it formed into an eye. Was this an acceleration of time?

The speed that molecules travel causes changes in their molecular structure. I am not a scientist but speed is how fast (time) things travel through space. Did people travel through time and space in Jesus time?

- Jesus walked on water – Did molecules travel faster and form a solid water surface at his command? Was that a miracle?
- Jesus was on the other side of the Sea of Galilee instantly. Was that time travel? Is that a miracle?
- Elijah was translated to heaven. He didn't die an earthly death but was taken up to heaven. Is that time travel? Is that a miracle?
- Jesus died. His spirit left his body and he visited hell and took the keys of hell back, then returned to his body and walked the earth 3 more days. Were these miracles and was time involved?
- Phillip, one of the apostles, was caught up in the spirit and was immediately found in another city 25 miles away. That is a miracle of time!

We can't limit God!!! He is a supernatural God. If he can create time, he can change and modify time through redeeming it for his purposes.

God's Promises Were Kept Through Miracles

Let's take the story of Caleb. Caleb was sent into the Promise Land to bring back a report to Moses of the weakness and strength of the enemy and a description of the place God had promised his people. Caleb was 40 years old when he went to the promise land for the first time. He brought back a good report; one not full of fear of the enemy but one of confidence that with God's help, the enemy could be defeated and they could possess the promise God had given them when they left Egypt. The other men's reports were that the enemy was too powerful, and because of their lack of faith, those without faith in God didn't get to possess and enjoy the land. As a result, all the Israelites were sent out into the wilderness for 40 years. But because of Caleb's trust in the Lord, he was honored and allowed to complete his assignment to enter into the promise land 40 years later. After the years of wandering in the desert, a new generation of Israelites returned to Canaan and with Joshua and Caleb, entered and received the promises given to their fathers while they were still in Egypt. Caleb by this time was 85 years old and he described himself like this. "I am as strong as I was the day Moses sent me out. I am as strong as ever in battle." Joshua 14:11 In order to fight the battles and receive his inheritance, his 85 year old body was as strong as or stronger than when he was 40. In order to accomplish his destiny, God stopped the natural aging process, both physically and mentally, so Caleb could complete his assigned task of possessing the promise land. It was for God's purposes that the miracles occurred. God says in Psalms 103:6, *"I (God) make everything come out right; I put victims back on their feet."* Caleb was a victim of the men who went to survey the land. These men had no faith in God and brought back a bad report, but Caleb said, we can take it. And for Caleb's faith, God honored his promise to Caleb and allowed him to fight and possess the land with the physical strength he had in the earlier part of his life. God renewed his youth in order to meet his destiny. That's a miracle and it was accomplished by a miracle of time redemption!

At 64, when God promised Sarah she would provide Abram with a child, she was well past her child-bearing age. And it still took another 24 years, making Sarah 88 years old when Isaac would be born. It was a miracle! Both Sarah and Abram's bodies and souls were renewed in order for them to accomplish God's plan. Time didn't matter to God. Why? Because God created time and he knows how to redeem time.

King Hezekiah was told by Isaiah, the prophet, that God had revealed to him that he was going to die. The king wasn't ready to die, so he went to God and said:

> *"Remember, O God, who I am, what I've done! I've lived an honest life before you, my heart's been true and steady, I've lived to please you, I've lived for your approval." I Kings 20:3*

God had compassion and told Isaiah to tell the king that he was going to heal him and give him 15 more years to live. To show King Hezekiah that the message was true and from God, the king asked Isaiah for a sign proving that this was a truth from God. God answered with a choice for the king to see the shadow on the sun dial to move forward by 10 degrees or move back by 10 degrees. The degrees on the sundial moved as the sun moved. He chose to make the shadow go back 10 degrees and it did. It did not matter to God, whether time would go forward or backward because he could stop the sun's movement in order to stop time, to prove to one man that he was the God of that universe.

God redeems time for his purposes. Time is not our enemy or a curse to us. Changes need to become our friend. Redeeming the time is not to be taken lightly but to be considered a blessing. Since Jesus gave us the authority he had, we have the same authority over time. We need to make it work for us. This is not a toy or magic for our own pleasures, but it is used for the manifestation of God's glory. It is for God's assignments; in order for his destined purposes to be manifest that we can enter into the miracle realm. We don't have to understand it but when needed, we need not be afraid to use the faith, power and authority that God has given us.

God is willing and able to do anything that makes his "will" happen. And we must walk in the Spirit to know his will and purposes. All of these stories show that it was in God's will for them to happen. The characters that were involved all walked closely with God and desired to be in his will. If we strive to walk in his presence and follow whatever God tells us to do, that obedience will result in miracles!

Personal Application of Time Redemption

While I was studying time redemption, God walked me through several experiences that proved to me that time redemption was for kingdom use. I would like to share a couple of my experiences to help you understand how this might be used in your everyday kingdom life.

Economic Recession of 2008

September 2008 was a memorable time for me. I was preparing for a much needed vacation to Paris, France. I am a real estate agent and had been awarded this trip for two people, for selling a beautiful new home from one of the top builders in my area. What a surprise it was to win such a wonderful trip. Two days before my flight, it was announced that Hurricane IKE would be hitting the coast near our city. My home in Houston, Texas is less than 2 miles from the coast of Galveston Bay and so these announcements always cause confusion to the area as everyone begins to prepare for a possible disaster. Because this was an extremely large storm, many airline flights would be cancelled as the airports began to prepare for the storm.

I thought OK, I'll just enjoy a few extra days in Paris and proceeded to move my trip up a couple of days. My sister, also a real estate agent, and I were on the last flight out of Houston that morning; leaving behind the fears of what the hurricane would do to our area. I was having a very successful year in real estate and had an extra-large number of closings scheduled upon my return. Hurricanes can cause havoc to our business because heavy winds blow down trees and take roofs off houses, and the large amount of rain that falls during the storm causes flooding to the homes in our area. These storms almost always cause delays and cancellations of home sales, but there was nothing that we could do. We would face the damage of the storm when we returned.

The storm blew over the area with minimum damage, praise God. But a greater disaster was on the horizon - one that no one expected or knew about. The great fall of the Stock Market, September 17, 2008. While in Paris, I kept my business hat on and tried to keep up with the economic news of the downturn as I wondered how it would affect my business. I returned after the wonderful trip and worked diligently to close as many deals as possible and was able to hold everyone together with only slight delays. The day after the last closing occurred, I realized that my phone had completely stopped ringing and that the future was about to display itself.

I realized I was in unknown financial territory and as a single lady, if I didn't get business, I might be in for great financial struggles. I sat down and surveyed my situation and stopped all unnecessary expenditures and tightened my belt. I began to pray for wisdom and for fear not to take me over. And just like a woman, in jest, I prayed that my make-up would last as long as I need it to and the shoes on my feet would not need to be replaced until I was financially stable again. I remember thinking, how vain is this, but I also remember thinking the future could be changing and I had to do my best to make it financially. Now, I know God always provides for us and I claimed all my Biblical promises and God did provide. The funny thing about it was, when things did get tight, God provided but there was no extra money for make-up and shoes. Almost four years later, the economy of the US started improving and when I looked back, I never had to buy make-up or shoes. And I was still able to look my best every day.

It was after this time that God started to reveal the deep truths of redeeming time and the story of the Israelites' clothes and shoes was brought to my attention and I realized I had experienced the same miracle they had.

Computer Disaster

In today's world, we are very dependent on our computers. In 2013, I was typing on my computer and without any warning, my business computer went completely dead. I wasn't overly concerned because I had two hard drives—one to work on and one to back-up everything I did. Since I had some business proposals due, I quickly took the computer over to our local tech company. What they told me was that the hard drive had crashed and everything on the computer was gone. When I asked about the second drive, they said it was also completely empty.

In that moment, I was terrified. I cried out to God and asked him to recover and restore all my data. The computer tech said <u>ALL</u> of my business system, pictures, and personal records were gone. The tech must be wrong! I believed God would honor my prayer and I asked what could be done. All the tech person could offer me was to send both of the drives off to a specialist, who had a machine that could recover anything if it could be found. The cost was expensive, but not as expensive as losing 15 years of files on the drive. They rushed it across Houston and three days later, I received a call from the experts. They could not find a trace of anything on either drive. I cried out in prayer again, and I heard in my spirit to have the two drives sent back to me. So I called the specialist back and he overnighted the drives back to my office. That afternoon, I was talking with my book-keeper, who said she had a wonderful new machine that allowed her to retrieve data off a lot of her customers' computers when they crashed. She offered to try and recover mine. I was still walking in faith that God could retrieve my data, so I took it to her to see if she could find anything; only to hear the same results.

Why would God tell me to have the hard drives returned to me and then get the same result? The one thing the bookkeeper did say, was that the second drive, which was meant for back-ups was just like new and if I would replace it back into the case of the old computer, it would be just like a new computer with a good hard drive. I had already purchased a new computer and had accepted the fact that everything had been lost, but I allowed the drive to go back in the case of the original computer. Back at the office, I had a message from my son asking me if I had an old computer he could use for a new business venture he was doing. I said sure and thought maybe that was why God had me put the drive back into the computer again. You can imagine my shock when my son called me the next day and said when he opened my computer up, all my files were there! Three professional techs had told me there was nothing on either of the drives; but, GOD!!! What I asked and believed for was redeemed because he wanted to show me that his principles do work. By standing in faith and believing his principle, ALL was recovered. God showed me how the principle of redeeming time works today for his purposes. Don't be afraid, we can perform miracles just as Jesus did, if we will act on his Word!

> *"Answer this question: Does the God who lavishly provides you with his own presence, His Holy Spirit, working things in your lives you could never do for yourselves, does he do these things because of your strenuous moral striving or because you trust him to do them in you?...Is it not obvious to you that persons who put their trust in Christ (not persons who put their trust in the law!) are like Abraham: children of faith?" Galatians 3:5, 7*

Saving my Life for his Purpose!

I saved the best story for last! It was the end of the Christmas holiday season and my daughter's husband's job was changing; resulting in a move to Dallas from Houston for their family. They had a large three story home and with my grandchildren being 8 and 10 years old they had lots of stuff to pack. It was a huge packing job. The move was emotionally hard on me, so I worked very hard to make the holiday season a special time with great memories of their Houston family.

Everything was packed and the moving van was pulling out with the two family cars, kids and dog following it to Dallas. After a sad good-bye, it was my job to stay behind and clean the house and get it ready to start showing it for rental. Like the rest of the country, the recession had been hard on our housing market and they were going to have to wait for the return of market value to sell it. I personally was hoping that this was only a short little move away and they would be returning in a few years to the two-year old dream home.

It was late that evening when the cleaning was complete and I had little time for rest because I needed to be in Dallas by noon the next day to help them start unpacking and setting up there. I couldn't sleep so at about 3 o'clock in the morning, I got up and headed for Dallas; a 5 hour drive to the new home. I was pleasantly surprised how fast the drive was going when I hit the half-way point at Fairfield. Then on the north side of town, my body began to crash from the lack of sleep and the tiring work of the day before. I had just passed the last place to get gas or coffee, so I decided I would drive the 40 miles to the next town and then stop and take a rest there.

The next thing I remember was waking up to a sign saying "cars to the right and trucks to the left". It was a roadside rest stop! It was as if someone else was driving my car and before I even touched the steering wheel, the car had stopped in a parking space. I looked around at all the cars and drivers taking naps and resting. Where was I? How did I get there? Truck drivers say the time right before sunrise is the hardest time to stay awake for them and this rest stop proved it. It was completely full of cars and 18-wheel trucks trying to recover from the dangerous night drive. I knew I had just experienced a miracle because I had no knowledge of how I got to the rest stop. I began crying and thanking God for my safety. After realizing how much danger I had been in and how God had truly saved me from death, I realized I felt completely refreshed. I started the car again and continued the second half of the drive completely energized.

I didn't tell anyone about the incident, who would believe me and besides, my daughter would just worry about me. She had enough to worry about getting her family settled. A few days later after my family was settled in, it was time to return home. The drive home was the first time I had stopped to think in depth about what had happened on the drive up. As I approached the rest stop from the opposite direction, I starting praising God again for his protection and for saving me from "death" on the drive up to Dallas. I knew that there was no way that I had driven that stretch of the road so; I began questioning God about it. God quickened me to review the area where it happened. The first thing I did was see the location of the sign, "cars to the right" and realized there was a sharp split where the feeder entered the parking area. I looked down the road and saw the feeder went a long distance and rose over a hill and dropped into a valley where there was a long bridge over a low river bed before it reached where it had split off the busy I-45 freeway that ran between Houston and Dallas. The feeder continued on for about 2 more miles before it finally intersected the busy highway again. I realized then, that I didn't remember any of this nor had I ever seen the sign that night that said "Rest Stop Ahead" so travelers could prepare to pull off the freeway. It was over 20 miles to the place where the sleepiness had caused me to black out in the town of Fairfield, where I finally remembered passing the last place to get coffee 3 nights before. After that everything was clear again and I had complete memory of the previous drive from Houston.

I know I did not do that drive! I can't tell you how long I was asleep at the wheel, but I know that it was not just a brief few seconds and somehow it could have been as long as 20-30 minutes of normal drive time on a busy interstate highway with other cars and trucks driving to their locations. You noticed I said normal drive time. God had redeemed time for me that night; there is no doubt in my mind that I did not drive that 25 miles. I don't know if my car was placed in a time capsule or an angel drove it down the road...all I know is that I got there safely. It was a miracle and God quickened my spirit that it was "redemption of time."

TIME is Important in Kingdom Life

I'm not going to try to explain it, but I do want to tell you that time is one of God's tools in his kingdom. *Time is based on movement of **light***...The sun and the moon were created by God to create a way of measuring and documenting time. By definition in the Bible, time can be redeemed; and redeeming means stopping, suspending, reversing and/or accelerating time for God's purposes. Spiritual things are revealed to us on a need-to-know basis when God thinks we need to know them! "God's purposes" causes spiritual truths to be revealed or illuminated to us.

"God is Light" and the purpose of light is to illuminate so we can see. Is it coincidental that in the Gospel of John, he describes Jesus is this way?

> *"The Word was first...God presented the Word. The Word was God, in readiness for God from day one. Everything was created through him; nothing—not one thing!—came into being without him. What came into existence was Life, and the Life was* ***LIGHT*** *to live by. The LIFE-****LIGHT*** *blazed out of the darkness and the darkness couldn't put it out...There once was a man, named John sent by God to point out the LIFE-****LIGHT****. John was not the* ***LIGHT****; he was there to show the way to the* ***LIGHT****. The LIFE-****LIGHT*** *was the real thing: Every person entering Life he brings into* ***LIGHT****...*
>
> *This is the crisis we're in: GOD-****LIGHT*** *streamed into the world, but men and women everywhere ran for the darkness. They went for the darkness because they were not really interested in pleasing God. Everyone who makes a practice of doing evil, addicted to denial and illusion, hates GOD-****LIGHT*** *and won't come near it, fearing a painful exposure. But anyone working and living in truth and reality welcomes GOD-****LIGHT*** *so the work can be seen for the God-work it is...Jesus once again addressed them; "I am the world's* ***LIGHT****. No one who follows me stumbles around in the darkness. I provide plenty of light to live in...For as long as I am in the world, there is plenty of* ***LIGHT****. I am the world's* ***LIGHT****...Are there not twelve hours of daylight? Anyone who walks in daylight doesn't stumble because there's plenty of* ***LIGHT*** *from the sun. Walking at night, he might very well stumble because he can't see where he's going (because there is no* ***LIGHT*** *in him)...*
>
> *Jesus said, 'For a brief time still, the* ***LIGHT*** *is among you. Walk by the* ***LIGHT*** *you have so darkness doesn't destroy you. If you walk in darkness, you don't know where you're going. Now you have the* ***LIGHT****. Then the* ***LIGHT*** *will be within you, and shining through your lives. You'll be children of* ***LIGHT****.'...*
>
> *I am* ***LIGHT*** *that has come into the world so that all who believe in me won't have to stay any longer in the dark." John 1:1-9, 8:12, 9:5, 11:9, 12:35-36, 12:46*

Isn't God wonderful? Only he could write a whole book in the Bible to tell the story of Jesus's life on the earth. Within that book, you can extract the Scriptures that have the word **"light"** in them to get a clear definition of who he is: "light" and how "light" works in the believer's life.

God is **LIGHT** and Jesus, his son, came to earth to show the **LIGHT** to the world. Those who follow the light would:

- Please God, the Father of Light
- Have plenty of light to illuminate their lives
- Not stumble and fall from the favor of God
- No evil would destroy them
- Let the light shine through to others so they can discover the light
- Have eternal life

The facts are:

- **Jesus is light**. *"I am **LIGHT** that has come into the world so that all who believe in me won't have to stay any longer in the dark." John 12:4-6*
- **Blood is made of congealed light.** *"The Word became flesh and blood...John pointed him out and called, 'This is the One! The One I told you was coming after me but in fact was ahead of me. He has always been ahead of me, has always had the first word." John 1:14*
- **To have life, you must have blood.** *"For the life of the flesh (is) in the blood: and I have given it to you upon the altar to make an atonement for your souls: for it (is) the blood (that) maketh an atonement for the soul." Leviticus 17:11 (KJV)*
- **We are the sons and daughters of Jesus; therefore, we are the lights to the world.** *"Ye are the **light** of the world. A city that is set on a hill cannot be hid." Matthew 5:14 (KJV)*

Science shows that all matter is congealed light. This light isn't like from the sun or a lamp but is waves of energy. Science says all energy waves are light. How does this compare to what the Scriptures say?

- What both the Scriptures and science are saying, is that when you get to the very source of LIFE, there is light and light measures time. Just as all Scripture points to Jesus, so does all science.

- There is an old saying, "When the student is READY, the teacher will APPEAR!" It's just a matter of how much you, the student, wish to study the information and ask God for truth and revelation of how the two work together. Remember, *I am **LIGHT** that has come into the world so that all who believe in me won't have to stay any longer in the dark. John 8:12*

If you remember, when God said, *"Let there be light; and there was light"*, in Genesis 1:3. When was this? On which day? The sun, moon and stars had not yet been created until the fourth day. So what is this light (both seen and unseen)? Is this a Kingdom Mystery? Will God reveal to you a deeper meaning of light and time if you ask?

Jesus said,

> *"I am the **light** of the world: he that follows me shall not walk in darkness, but shall have the **light** of life". John 8:12*

Paul, the apostle of Jesus said.

> *"For everything, absolutely everything, above and below, visible and invisible, rank after rank after rank of angels—everything got started in him and finds its purpose in him. He was there before any of it came into existence and holds it all together right up to this moment." Colossians 1:16-17*

Life, light and **time** all are inter-related to each other. The Bible says in Hosea, "for lack of knowledge we perish" and in Genesis, "we are to take dominion over the work of his hands." One work of his hand is the creation of light and time. If we lack the knowledge of how we can take the authority over his creation of time, we diminish our effective use of time for God's kingdom purposes. We must get a revelation of the principle of "time redemption" for God's purposes. Revelation does not usually just fall on us, but it does come when we get passionate for God to reveal his deeper truths. Remember, God gives us revelation knowledge for his purposes to be fulfilled.

We are never too old, too smart, or too spiritual for God to give us new revelation. And when he does, we should thank the Lord with all of our soul and all that is within us; thank him for his gift of knowledge, wisdom and revelation. Then use it for God's purposes and walk forward in our assignment and destiny using what he gave us. If we do, then God says in Psalms 103 that he will:

1. Forgive all our iniquities
2. Heal all our diseases
3. Redeem all of life's destructions
4. Crown us with loving kindness and tender mercies
5. Satisfy our mouth (our words) with good things
6. Renew our youth like the eagles

We must keep our souls fixed on God and his purposes. His Word, his Holy Spirit and the teaching of Jesus and the kingdom, will keep our lives directed and heading toward destiny. Time is not our enemy; it is our friend, if we understand it is a tool in the kingdom. See to it you take authority over time and use the authority cautiously and purposely by walking in the Spirit

A Prayer to Activate the Principle of Time

God, help me to use time correctly. I want to put time to work for me. I don't want to be in bondage to time because there is not enough time for everything I need to do. But instead, give me freedom… by making it multiply and showing me how to use my time for your service in your kingdom.

I come against time-stealers in my life and I stop Satan from using them for advancement of his kingdom. I ask you to lengthen my days and give me long life for your use, your glory, and your kingdom.

In Jesus' name. Amen

Kingdom Thinking

Knowing that principles of redemption and restoration are important, name 5 ways God has restored/redeemed your personal life, since you became a Christian? How did these restorations change your life?

What is Jesus' number one purpose in the Kingdom of God?

Name 2 examples of "time travel" in the Bible. Do you believe we can travel forward or backward in time today? Why or why not? What is God's requirement for time travel and other miracles?

What are three things listed in Ephesians 5 you need to do to live successfully in the Kingdom of God?

What is the kingdom call to God's people today? How does time fit into your calling?

How do life, light and time relate to each other?

Who is the "Light of the World" and why?

Keys to the Kingdom

- If Jesus' ministry had a theme, it would be restoring mankind to God's perfect order.
- Remember, be wise and by faith, use our knowledge to move the mountains in our life in Jesus name.
- Jesus will return to earth for his Church but the Church is not ready. It is our job to get ready!
- Jesus did everything he saw his Father doing. And we are called to do the same, by walking in the Spirit.
- Redeeming time and using time wisely is a supernatural principle.
- The number one principle in the kingdom is obedience to the "will of God". If we walk in God's will, it will lengthen our days and add peace to our lives.
- We must live a Spirit-filled life, which is necessary to accomplish God's destiny in our lives and to perform miracles like Jesus did.
- Time redemption and all miracles are for God's purposes only.
- We must use the faith, power and authority God has given us to see miracles performed.
- Time is important in the Kingdom of God.
- Jesus is LIGHT and he came into the world so that all who believe in him can be saved.
- Blood is congealed light and necessary for life, so we must understand the importance of blood.
- Jesus' blood gives us eternal life.
- Just as all Scriptures point to Jesus, so does all science.

Not My Will, but Yours

by Joy E. Miller

"Not My Will, but Yours" took over a year to paint. God gave me the challenge to paint a picture that would include Jesus at all the key locations of his death, resurrection and return to establish His Kingdom. It took some time to figure out how do that. The key locations are:

- The Garden of Gethsemane where Jesus surrendered his will over to His Father, also shows Peter, James and John who he took with him to support him in prayer while he waited for the soldiers to come arrest him.
- The City of Jerusalem, where he was on trial and unjustly sentenced to death. He was beaten and carried his cross to the streets to his crucifixion.
- The Hill of Golgotha (the skull) outside of the city where follows and family would witness his brave death.
- The grave where he would be buried with the angel that ministered to him after he rose from the dead and went to hell to take the keys to the kingdom from Satan.

Jesus return to earth to rapture his believers and establish the Millennium Age for his church. I knew it was complete when my youngest granddaughter at the age of 3, first saw the picture as she came into the studio and stopped in her tracks and said, "There is my Jesus"!

CHAPTER 9

Kingdom Mysteries

The change that we experience after our "born again" experience is more than a one-time experience...It is a process over our lifetime and possibly into eternity! We are "A Work in Progress". Joy Miller

In the time that we live in, the 21st century, we have seen so many changes that it has been hard for us to keep up with it all. The technology alone has been mind-boggling. My personal journey began in 1948, after World War II; being born into the "baby boomer generation". My Dad and Mom had married at 16 years old, left their home in Oklahoma and headed for California to find a better life. My dad's parents were tenant farmers and never owned their own land. They had 8 children and my dad, the third child, was the first child to leave rural life. My mom's family lived in several small towns and moved around the countryside following the pipelines of a fledgling industry as it developed...the oil and gas industry of the 1930-40's. Both families were hard workers and did whatever needed to be done to survive during the Great Depression and the re-building of America after two world wars.

After many dead-end jobs on the west coast, Dad heard about a steel company that needed workers in Houston, Texas. He and my pregnant mother, headed to Texas, hoping Texas would provide a better life. Dad, now 17 years old, had to lie about his age to even get a job. The company needed strong young men that were willing to shovel the raw materials into the hot-hot furnaces that would melt together to form the steel used to build the great cities of America. Talk about a devilish job! The temperatures and humility of the Texas coast along with the heat of those furnaces would make hell almost melt. There was no air conditioning at that time and the men worked shift work, alternating from days to nights, so no one would have to endure the extreme temperatures of the hot Texas days without sharing the somewhat cooler nights.

I remember going out with Dad and collecting moss from the local trees so he could build a make-shift air conditioner. He built a wooden frame the size of the window and inserted chicken-wire where you could drape tree moss. He then ran a water hose to the window and dripped water on the moss while a fan blew air through the moss on my dad as he lay in his bed trying to sleep. This would slightly cool the air to give him some relief so he could return to the hot furnaces for his next shift at the steel mill. There was no relief from that Texas heat except the slightly cooler days of the Texas winters.

Our car was an outdated Model A with no floor-board and when he took Mom to the hospital to have me, he had to drag his feet on the dirt road to slow the car down. I tell this story in order to help you understand what the average lifestyle of the 1940's and 50's was like for a working man. When I was 4 years old, my dad bought our first TV, and in 1957, I remember Dad bringing home one of the first cars that had an air conditioner. Dad was very progressive for a man of the 50's and was determined to take advantage of all the new technology that was developing. In 1966, when I graduated from high school, the dirt farmer from Oklahoma was able to send me to Baylor University so I could have a better life. My parents had come a long way in 18 years. Dad had become the General Manager of the steel mill and I left home to get a first rate college education.

Since then, it has been like a whirlwind, as our society truly began to mature. As a result of President Kennedy's decision to put a man on the moon before 1970, the technological generation developed fast. I have been very fortunate to have a family that taught me "We can live the American dream and be whatever our minds can dream if we work for it."

I was in real estate in the early 1990's when the first mobile phones came out on the market. I called it the "Phone in a Box". It was housed in a large purse-like bag and I remember taking it home and trying to call a friend across the street without success. Technology continued to get better. It was a matter of choice to continue to grow with it. Ever since then, I have tried to stay current with the development of technology, but even more important, to stay sane as the information age caused continually changes.

My grandchildren don't have these problems; they have no fear of technology and at very young ages, they pick up a piece of technology and seem to know how to do all the things that took me 20 years to figure out. Recently, I went to a presentation telling the leaders in my industry where this technological generation is heading. In the next few years, everything that we have today will seem like a wooden wheel next to a spaceship. The changes coming will revolutionize us to new levels. This brief history of technology will help you understand that everything may be changing and developing at a rapid speed around us, but our God is the same as he has always been. He uses the same principles today that Jesus taught during his time on the earth in 30 AD.

Many Christians are frustrated in their personal growth and their relationship with God. But, God is patient to wait on us to make permanent changes from the inside outward, which will cause us to develop from our spirit man so others will see Jesus living in us. Our development is determined by our "will" and our willingness to change. His method for changing us into his image and character is not done with technology and other modern teaching methods, but is accomplished by teaching us the same kingdom principles that Jesus taught through life lessons and parables. The Bible says, *"Jesus doesn't change—yesterday, today, tomorrow, he's always totally himself." (Hebrews 13:8).* God wants us to make the lifestyle changes needed to be godly and then remain consistent to living them daily. If we do, he can then allow, *"All his blessings to come down on you and spread out beyond you because you have responded to the voice of God, your God." Deuteronomy 28:2-11*

What are these blessings?

- *God's blessing inside the city, God's blessing in the country* (Blessing where ever you are.)
- *God's blessing on your children, the crops of your land, the young of your livestock, the calves of your herds, the lambs of your flocks*. (Blessing on everything that is yours.)
- *God's blessing on your basket and bread bowl*. (Blessing on everything you purchase and eat.)
- *God's blessings on your coming in, and going out*. (Blessing wherever you go.)
- *God will defeat your enemies who attack you. They'll come at you on one road and run away on seven roads.* (Blessings of protection from your enemy.)
- *God will order a blessing on your barns and workplaces; he'll bless you in the land that God, your God, is giving you.* (Blessing on your job and home that he has given you.)

- *God will form you as a people holy to him, just as he promised you, if you keep the commandments of God, your God and live the way he has shown you.* (Blessing on your family.)
- *All the people on earth will see you living under the name of God and hold you in respectful awe.* (People will respect you for who you are.)
- *God will lavish you with good things; children from your womb, offspring from your animals, and crops from your land, the land that God promised your ancestors that he would give you.* (Bless and multiply everything you own with good things.) Based on Deuteronomy 28:1-11

God's Word is designed to produce life and peace within us and, by studying his Word and obeying it; we can't help but mature in God's principles which will result in blessings. Our faith will become stronger and stronger because, *"Faith comes by hearing, and hearing by the Word of God." Romans 10:17.* God is in control and no matter how fast our world is changing around us; his kingdom principles will continually impact our growth. We must study kingdom principles if we want to see these changes and his blessing in our lives!

Kingdom Economics

Addition and Division in the Kingdom

"May God himself, the God who makes everything holy and whole, make you holy and whole, put you together--spirit, soul and body—and keep you fit for the coming of our Master, Jesus Christ." 1 Thessalonians 5:23

Humans were created to be like God. God is one God; revealing himself in three different ways.

1. God Almighty-the creator-soul
2. Jesus Christ-Son of God and Savior of our soul-body
3. Holy Spirit-our guide and teacher-spirit

Just as God is divided into three parts, he made man and divided him into three parts: spirit, soul and body. For God to be complete and for man to be complete, both must have all three parts added together to be one.

OUR SPIRIT is the real person, who we are; our personality. It is the spirit of man that God matures into the person he made us to be. When we receive salvation, God awakens the spirit in us and begins to change us from the inside out. He not only awakens the spirit in us but also seals us for himself.

> *"Whatever God has promised gets stamped with the 'Yes' of Jesus. In him, this is what we preach and pray, the great Amen, God's yes and our yes together, gloriously evident. God affirms us, making us a sure thing in Christ, putting his yes within us. By his Spirit* (Holy Spirit)*, he has stamped us with his eternal pledge—a sure beginning of what he is destined to complete...It's what we trust in but don't yet see that keeps us going...Now we look inside, and what we see is that anyone united with the Messiah gets a fresh start, is created new. The old life is gone; a new life burgeons! Look at it! 2 Corinthians 1:20-22, 5:17*

God stamped or sealed us for his purposes with his signet ring (his personal mark); for our preservation from now, while we are in the Kingdom of God on earth, to the time we reside in his heavenly kingdom for eternity. From the moment we accepted Jesus as our Savior, God saw us complete and mature. He does not leave us in an immature state where other people are our teachers; but he matures us and teaches us through the Holy Spirit.

Colossians 2:10-19, tells us how God thinks of us and matures us.

> *"When you come to God, that fullness comes together for you, too. His power extends over everything. Entering into this fullness is not something you figure out or achieve. It's not a matter of being circumcised or keeping a long list of laws. No, you're already in-insiders—not through some secretive initiation rite but rather through what Christ has already gone through for you, destroying the power of sin. If it's initiation ritual you're after, you've already been through it by submitting to baptism. Going under the water was a burial of your old life, coming up out of it was a resurrection, God raising you from the dead as he did Christ. When you were stuck in your old sin—dead life, you were incapable of responding to God. God brought you alive—right along with Christ! Think of it! All sins forgiven, the slate wiped clean, the old arrest warrant cancelled and nailed to Christ's cross. He stripped all the spiritual tyrants in the universe of their sham authority at the*

> *Cross and marched them naked through the streets. So don't put up with anyone pressuring you in details of diet, worship services, or holy days. All those things are mere shadows cast before what was to come; the substance is Christ. Don't tolerate people who try to run your life, ordering you to bow and scrape, insisting that you join the obsession with angels and that you seek out visions. They're a lot of hot air, that's all they are. They're completely out of touch with the source of life, Christ, who puts us together in one piece, whose very breath and blood flow through us. He is the head and we are the body. We can grow up healthy in God only as he nourishes us."*

OUR SOUL is our mind, our will and our emotions. This is where we have our learning capacity and where God teaches us his wisdom and knowledge and adds to our earthly knowledge. The soul (mind) must line-up with the "spirit man" to accomplish God's destiny. It is in the soul (mind), that the battles with Satan take place. It is the battlefield where God and Satan fight for our maturity and eternal salvation.

> *"This is no afternoon athletic contest that we'll walk away from and forget about in a couple of hours. This is for keeps, a life-or-death fight to the finish against the Devil and all his angels. Be prepared. You're up against far more than you can handle on your own. Take all the help you can get, every weapon God has issued, so that when it's all over but the shouting you'll still be on your feet." Ephesians 6:12-13*

If we submit our mind, will and emotions over to God, God tells us the battles are his and he always wins over sin and he will gently correct our thinking, control our will and calm our emotions. It is by God renewing our mind that others see the changes in us and where God's light shines out to them. We must submit our soul (mind) to God's will!

> *"So here's what I want you to do. God helping you. Take your everyday, ordinary life—your sleeping, eating, going–to-work, and walking around life—and place it before God as an offering. Embracing what God does for you is the best thing you can do for him. Don't become so well-adjusted to your culture that you fit into it without even thinking. Instead, fix your attention on God. You'll be changed from the inside out. Readily recognize*

what he wants from you, and quickly respond to it. Unlike the culture around you, always dragging you down to its level of immaturity. God brings the best out of you, develops well-formed maturity in you. I'm speaking to you out of deep gratitude for all that God has given me, and especially as I have responsibilities in relation to you. Living then, as every one of you does, in pure grace, it's important that you not misinterpret yourselves as people who bring this goodness to God. No, God brings it all to you. The only accurate way to understand ourselves is by what God is and by what he does for us, not by what we are and what we do for him." Romans 12:1-3

We tend to think and meditate on who we are, what is important to us and how it affects us. That is not God's way in the kingdom. He wants us to think, meditate and submit to who he is; and what is important to him and his way of thinking. And how do we know his way of thinking? By studying and meditating on his Words—the Bible. It is hard to live in this world and not conform to what is going on around us and to the evil and ugly ways of it. We went go to God's Word, read it, meditated on it and allowed God to change their way of thinking. God even tells us what we are to think about. Paul, the apostle of God, instructed us in Philippians 4:1 like this:

"My dear, dear friends! I love you so much. I do want the very best for you. You make me feel such joy, fill me with such pride. Don't waver. Stay on track, steady in everything". How did Paul instruct the people to do it?

- PRAY about everything.
- CELEBRATE God all day, every day. I mean, REVEL in him.
- DON'T FRET OR WORRY. Instead let petitions and praise shape your worries into prayers.
- BE CONTENT whatever your circumstances.
- BE HAPPY with little as with much.
- MAKE IT THROUGH EVERYTHING through CHRIST who strengthens YOU.

"Summing it all up friends. I say you'll do best by filling your minds and meditating on things TRUE, NOBLE, REPUTABLE, AUTHENTIC, COMPELLING, GRACIOUS—THE BEST, NOT THE WORST, THE BEAUTIFUL NOT THE UGLY; THINGS TO PRAISE, NOT THINGS TO CURSE. Put into practice what you learned from me, what you heard and saw and realized. Do that, and God who makes

everything work together, will work you into his most excellent harmonies." Philippians 4:8-9

You can be sure that God will take care of everything you need, his generosity exceeds anything we could imagine and he promise us that he *"will supply all your needs according to his riches in Jesus Christ." Philippians 4:19 KJ*

Our thoughts affect our attitudes and moods. When we submit to "our thoughts" instead of God's, we are miserable and this usually results in making those around us miserable. But if we meditate on God's kingdom principles, we find that:

> *"God's wisdom is something mysterious that goes deep into the interior of his purposes. You don't find it lying around on the surface. It's not the latest message, but more like the oldest—what God determined as the way to bring out his best in us, long before we ever arrived on the scene. The experts of our day haven't a clue about what this eternal plan is. If they had, they wouldn't have killed the master of the God-designed life on a cross. That's why we have this Scripture text. No one's ever seen or heard anything like this (God's Word). Never so much as imagined anything quite like it—what God has arranged for those who love him. But you've seen and heard it because God by his Spirit has brought it out into the open before you. The Spirit, not content to flit around on the surface, dives into the depths of God, and bring out what God planned all along." 1 Corinthians 2:7-12*

God skillfully finessed the changes in our thinking by his Holy Spirit (the third part of God). God by his Holy Spirit activated his wisdom and knowledge, in cooperation with our spirit, to change our soul (mind) into his way of thinking. We don't have to rely on the world's way of thinking! And we won't learn God's way in worldly schools and books—it is only revealed and taught to us by his Holy Spirit revealing it to us and us allowing it to change our thinking. Our spirit is born again when we accept Jesus as our Savior but our minds must be renewed through time as God changes us, as we submit to him. We can have the mind of Christ if we choose to.

Our Body is the third part of us. Our body is the house of our soul and spirit. God says our body is his earthly "Temple of God". He formed it from the dirt of the ground on the last day of creation. Physically, we are made from dirt and we are nurtured through the dirt. In other words, our food that keeps our body alive comes from the dirt. All forms of food God created have their origins from the dirt.

Plants are grown in the dirt and even our meat comes from animals known as "beast of the fields" and "birds of the air", which get their nutrition by eating plants that are grown in the dirt.

God provides the both food to sustain the physical body and "spiritual food" for the "spiritual temple" (our spirit and mind). Each are grounded and explained symbolically in one of Jesus' parables taught in Matthew 13. He used the growth patterns of plants that grow in dirt as a kingdom mystery.

Seed Time and Harvest

Subtraction and Multiplication

In these parables, Jesus personally explained how the gospels function during our present dispensation known as the "church age". The "church age" began with Jesus' earthly ministry, the last 3 years before his death and resurrection, and will continue until Jesus comes back for his church as described in Revelation.

During this time, Jesus challenges his followers with the "Great Commission"...

> *"Go out and train everyone you meet, far and near, in this way of life, making them disciples by baptism in the threefold name: Father, Son, and Holy Spirit. Then instruct them in the practice of all I have commanded you. I'll be with you as you do this, day after day after day, right to the end of the age."* Matthew 28:19-20

We, as Christians, are to spread the good news of the gospel to all the people of the world and spread kingdom truths throughout the earth. This will result in a "harvest" of believers who love and accept Jesus as their Savior.

As believers, while on earth, we are to grow into maturity and be prepared for Jesus' return for his church. The "end time harvest" occurs just before Jesus raptures all his believers both dead and alive in Christ to live with him for eternity. The harvest of believers will return with these other believers to earth with Jesus to establish the Millennial Age. This age will last for 1000 years after the earth has experience the seven years of Tribulation revealed in Revelations the last book of the Bible. In our present age, believers have had approximately 2000 years of sowing the seeds of faith into others. This has had mixed results. Let's explore a mysterious parable and see if we can understand Jesus' interpretation of the parable that he shared with his disciples. This will help us understand why we have not had better results in understanding and maturing in our own growth at times.

Jesus told the parable of "Seed Time and Harvest" in order to give a natural example that people of the time could understand. He addressed the crowd of people who had been following him like this:

> *"What do you make of this? A farmer planted seed. As he scattered the seed, some of it fell on the road, and birds ate it. Some fell in the gravel, it sprouted quickly but didn't put down roots, so when the sun came up it withered just as quickly. Some fell in the weeds; as it came up, it was strangled by the weeds. Some fell on good earth, and produced a harvest beyond his wildest dreams." Matthew 13:3-9*

The key to parables is understanding its meaning; however, without God's perfect timing we will not have any understanding. The revelation is understood only when God's, through his Holy Spirit, believes an individual is mature enough for the next growth step in the kingdom. It is like a promotion based on our relationship with God. The mystery is only divulged to believers when they are ready! It has been hidden from ungodly and wicked men; therefore, this parable is known as a "Kingdom Mystery".

The parable of "seed time and harvest" is such an important basic concept, that Jesus explained it like a building block to understanding all his other kingdom parables. It is imperative as Christians to understand it and it should be one of our first priority to study and comprehend it, in order to qualify for God's deeper truths. (This parable is so important that "Seed Time and Harvest" is taught in the book of Mark, also.)

> *"God's kingdom is like seed thrown on a field by a man who goes to bed and forgets about it. The seed sprouts and grows—he has no idea how it happens. The earth does it all without his help: first a green stem of grass, then a bud, then the ripened grain. When the grain is fully formed, he reaps—harvest time." Mark 2:26-29*

Jesus then goes on to explained how the kingdom works.

> *"You've been given insight into God's kingdom—you know how it works. But to those who can't see it yet, everything comes in stories, creating readiness,*

> *nudging them toward receptive insight. These are people whose eyes are open but don't see a thing, whose ears are open but don't understand a word, who avoid making an about-face and getting forgiven...Do you see how this story works? All my stories work this way.*
>
> *The farmer plants the Word. Some people are like the seed that falls on the hardened soil of the road. No sooner do they hear the Word than Satan snatches away what has been planted in them. But there is such shallow soil of character that when the emotions wear off and some difficulty arrives, there is nothing to show for it.*
>
> *The seed cast in the weeds represents the ones who hear the kingdom news but are overwhelmed with worries about all the things they have to do and all they want to get. The stress strangles what they heard and nothing comes of it." Mark 4:11-19*

Jesus first explains that parables are stories about how the kingdom works. Many believers are not ready for the deeper knowledge and just want to continue the same life that they have been leading. So many will read the story because it is easy reading, all the while God is planting his Word in them; hoping it will take root and encourage them to study, mediate and get a deeper meaning for themselves. Their eyes and ears may or may not be receptive to the truth or its meaning but by reading the parable, God will feed the "spirit man" in them. That is how the parable works. The WORD is the SEED. The Word is planted in soil (spirit) of man and each man's spirit receives it in a different way. Some let Satan steal the Word immediately, while others are a little more receptive, yet they let the worries of this world strangle the Word. Still others are ready to receive the Word and it finds good ground and the Word's roots go deep into their spirit and grows to maturity. God is willing to plant lots of seed in people in order to find the believers that will be receptive and allow the seed to grow and mature. God is not in a hurry. He will wait on us to be ready for deeper meanings and to hunger for more of him in our life. What kind of ground is in your spirit? God's word falls on all and he is looking for the *"good earth—those whose hearts seize the Word and hold on no matter what, sticking with it until there's a harvest".* *LUKE 8:15*

This parable is a natural, earthly example of how the kingdom works. Only one out of four people (25%) grow to maturity in the kingdom. The other three out of four people (75%) don't desire to grow and may only get it at all. They might get a little excited hearing the parable, yet have no follow through to reap the harvest of the seed in their life. It takes more than good intentions for you to reap the benefits of kingdom life. However, only by putting the kingdom principles to work in your life, will you reap maturity and blessings as a Jesus' followers. The result is that only 25% of the Christians will do the work necessary to be called a faithful follower of Jesus.

We must understand, each individual is responsible for themselves; to have "eyes to see and ears to hear." What does that mean?

Jesus continued on to explain...

> *"Are you listening to this? Really listening?"*

Even the disciples were confused about the parable of the seed and asked Jesus why he told his truths in stories? Jesus replied like this.

> *"You've been given insight into God's kingdom. You know how it works. Not everybody has this gift, this insight, it hasn't been given to them. Whenever someone has a ready heart for this, the insights and understandings flow freely. But if there is not readiness, any trace of receptivity soon disappears. That's why I tell stories: to create readiness, to nudge the people toward receptive insight. In their present state they can stare till doomsday and not see it, listen till they're blue in the face and not get it. I don't want Isaiah's forecast repeated all over again:*
>
> > *Your ears are open but you don't hear a thing.*
> >
> > *Your eyes are awake but you don't see a thing.*
>
> *The people are blockheads! They stick their fingers in their ears so they won't have to listen; they screw their eyes shut so they won't have to look, so they won't have to deal with me face-to-face and let me heal them.*
>
> *But you have God-blessed eyes—eyes that see! And God-blessed ears—ears that hear! A lot of people, prophets and humble believers among them, would have given anything to see what you are seeing, to hear what you are hearing, but never had the chance.* *Matthew 13:11-17*

Jesus was saying that many times people only want basic salvation. Many accept Jesus as their Savior and have eternal life but that is all they want. They choose not to go deeper with God; to the deeper mysteries in God's spiritual truths. They think they are content with life as it is...so God doesn't allow them to understand the depth of his Word until they are ready for more.

As we wake up and desire a deeper walk, God will reveal more truth to us. Jesus stated how blessed the disciples were to hear these truths from him directly but many would follow after his death; who would not get the chance to see and hear the Master tell the parables. The disciples heard the parable right from the mouth of Jesus, hearing kingdom mysteries yet were taking it for granted. We must always take God's Word seriously. We should never take it for granted! If we do, God will not allow us to have eyes to see or ears to hear the full truth of his words.

Four levels of Understanding

Jesus then goes on and explains the four levels of understanding saying:

Level 1 - *"Study this story of the farmer planting seed. When anyone hears news of the kingdom and doesn't take it in, it just remains on the surface, and so the Evil One comes along and plucks it right out of the person's heart. This is the seed the farmer scatters on the road."* *Matthew 13:18-19*

> This is the only level where Satan has any access to the believer. Satan's purpose is to steal from a believer's budding faith before it has time to grow stronger. Faith grows from hearing the word and Satan does everything he can to stop the young believer from studying and understanding the word. Therefore, stopping the seed from taking root. This is where you hear the baby Christian say, "I just don't understand the Bible; it's like Greek to me." It takes time for the mind to be renewed and transformed into God's way of thinking and it is only through time in the word that understanding develops and the door to the heart is opened to learning. This is a period of time when the word goes in one ear and out the other. Yet the more the new believer spends in the word, the quicker the root of the word will grow.

LEVEL 2 - *"The Seed cast in the gravel—this is the person who hears and instantly responds with enthusiasm. But there is no soil of character, and so when the emotions wear off and some difficulty arrives, there is nothing to show for it. Matthew 13:20-21*

This is the person who likes the sound of the anointed words of a teaching, yet he has no strong root of his own and he lets things of the past take control over him. Things like:

- Old religious teaching or traditions of men.
- Present sin in his life.
- Fear of persecution from others.
- Roots of bitterness and unforgiveness.
- Bad reports or hearsay have more influence than the truth.

This is when the believer begins to grow his own roots but the world still has a hold on him. These followers must make changes in their lives and realize that God's Word is "truth" and should be honored over all other opinions. Believers must remember, Satan is a liar and is willing to say anything to steal the truth from them. A person must grow deeper roots in God's Word and as they get stronger, the truth is harder to steal.

LEVEL 3 - *"The seed cast in the weeds is the person who hears the kingdom news, but weeds of worry and illusions about getting more and wanting everything under the sun strangle what was heard, and nothing comes of it." Matthew 12:22*

At this level most people stop their growth and allow things of this world to become more important. People lose focus on what is important or get busy trying to get ahead of others around them. Many ministers and other church leaders become people-pleasers or have too much pride in their own knowledge and wisdom. Many people stop listening to God's leadings and become people-helpers or educational junkies and go from meeting to meeting instead of doing things God's way. They stop taking the Word seriously and forget that they need God.

Level 4 – *"The seed cast on good earth is the person who hears and takes in the News, and then produces a harvest beyond his wildest dreams". Matthew 12:23*

The believer now hears the Word and believes and understands it. It is at this time that the believer becomes very fruitful. Yet the levels of growth continue to depend on the person's ability to give away what they have received. The purpose of bountiful harvest is to have more so you can give some wisdom and knowledge away, blessing others. The believer develops an attitude of less the world and more of God's best!

The roots go deeper now and the results are the abundant harvest because there is:

- Less cares of the world.
- Less weeds that stunt growth.
- Less hardness of heart but rather a heart of gratitude and giving.
- Less gravel or rocks to hinder growth into new levels.
- Less pride but more heart for others' spiritual growth.

WARNING - *"Put the seed in good earth—these are the good-hearts who seize the Word and hold on no matter what, sticking with it until there's a harvest. No one lights a lamp and then covers it with a washtub or shoves it under the bed. No, you set it up on a lamp stand so those who enter the room can see their way. We're not keeping secrets, we're telling them. We're bringing everything out into the open. So be careful that you don't become misers of what you hear. Generosity begets generosity. Stinginess impoverishes." LUKE 8:15-18*

We must continue to fight for the good soil so we can keep reaping. On this earth, we will never arrive at all knowledge and all wisdom; therefore, we can't just sit back and enjoy the fruit of our labors; we must give it away. We should always share what we learn with others. If not, we will become impoverished. It would be a shame if we did not share what God had shared with us.

Remember, God used kingdom math every day in the kingdom. If each level represents about 25% of the overall kingdom, God subtracted 75% of his kingdom's subjects to get to the 25% that will make a difference in the kingdom. It is this group that multiplies a harvest beyond their wildest dreams by giving the seeds away to others. These seeds will produce a harvest of fruit; some will have produced hundredfold, some sixty, some thirty (Matthew 13:23 KJ). The other 75% do not re-produce and do not reap the greater harvest.

Less is more to God. This is kingdom math which does not add up in our earthly world. Only a little, reproduces and causes the multiplication to manifested in the kingdom. God used it to bless those who do want to mature and who will give his message away. This cause the harvest and the multiplication of population growth in his kingdom.

Another place this principle works is in kingdom giving. The economy of the kingdom is based on his children giving away at least a tenth of all they receive. The other 90% is for our needs and enjoyment. God doesn't need the money—the kingdom's streets are paved with gold and the cattle on a thousand hills are the King's...but by giving a portion back to the kingdom, his 'kingdom economics' and kingdom blessings go in to effect. By us honoring God with our substance, trusting him for all of our needs and obeying his instruction for sowing and reaping; the kingdom principle of giving goes into effect by his followers giving a tithe. We then reap the results of the principle of seed time and harvest as mentioned in Mark 4:20. As we plant our financial substance with an understanding of the kingdom's way of multiplying and utilizing the principle of faith, it will produce a harvest that brings forth abundant fruit of its own kind; "some thirty fold, some sixty and some hundred." God encourages us to

> *"Bring your full tithe to the temple treasury so there will be ample provision in my Temple. Test me in this and see if I don't open up heaven itself to you and pour out blessings beyond your wildest dreams." Malachi 3:10.*

He promises us that he will open up the windows of heaven, and pour out such a blessing, that there shall not be room enough to receive it. This is a kingdom principle of <u>subtracting</u> from our substance and it <u>multiplying</u> back to us.

There are many other examples of this principle in the Bible. Abundance and multiplication are repeatedly seen in kingdom mathematics. The principles work because we are God's people and we are hidden in his Son, Jesus Christ. Satan has tried to steal kingdom math's blessing but all of these principles were recovered for us at Calvary and are now ours to benefit from in the Kingdom of God on earth. Jesus made it very simple when he said most people are not ready for his deeper truths:

> *"Your ears are open but you don't hear a thing.*
>
> *Your eyes are awake but you don't see a thing."*

Then he added: ***"But you have God-blessed eyes—eyes that see! And God-blessed ears—ears that hear!"*** *Mathew 13:16*

What kind of eyes and ears do you have? It is your decision how you see and hear!

Kingdom Thinking

Can you see changes in your life with the technological advancements of the last 5-10 years? Are these permanent changes or temporary changes and explain why?

List 5 areas you have experienced "spiritual" growth in the last few years. Are these permanent or temporary changes? Are you presently in a time of change? If so, how? Has Satan tried to steal these achievements from you? HOW?

Deuteronomy 28 is known as the chapter of Abraham's "blessings", given to him for hearing and obeying God. We are the spiritual children of Abraham and every blessing in that chapter can be claimed by us, if we will obey God too. Which blessing are you claiming today and why?

Name the three parts of man and connect each part to one of the three-part presentations of God.

Give the Apostle Paul's explanation of water baptism. Is this baptism necessary for salvation?

What did Paul instruct us to do in order to stay focused on God and not the things of this world?

What is the significance of dirt in creation and in parables?

What kind of ground is in your spirit? Will you let God's Word fall on good ground?

What are the four levels of subjects (believers) in the kingdom and what level are you on now? Where do you want to be? Are you willing to change?

Keys to the Kingdom

- God's methods for changing us into his image and character is not done with technology and other modern teaching methods but is accomplished by teaching us the kingdom principles.
- God is patient to wait on us to make permanent changes that will cause us to develop from our spirit man, outwardly, so others will see Jesus living in us.
- By God's Holy Spirit when we are saved, he has stamped us with his eternal pledge— to complete what he has started in us so we can reach our destiny that God planned for us before the beginning of time.
- It is in the soul (mind), that the battles with Satan take place. It is the battlefield where God and Satan fight for our maturity and eternal salvation.
- Through renewing our minds, we can have the mind of Christ.
- Parables are mysteries which hold hidden spiritual truths or secrets, generally only divulged to believers when they are ready to understand.
- Only one out of four people (25%) grow to maturity in the kingdom. The other three out of four people (75%) don't desire to grow and may only get a little excited hearing the parable yet have no follow through to reap the harvest of the seed in their life.
- Jesus made it very simple when he said most people are not ready for his deeper truths. But he is faithful to keep presenting the seed until we are ready!

God With Us

by Joy E. Miller

Christmas was approaching, and with it time to change the house décor for the holiday season. A blank, white canvas stared at me, defiant —daring me to paint. Then, in a flash across my artistic mind, "God with Us" and the meaning behind it appeared.

Not wanting to do a traditional Madonna and Baby Jesus, I saw a large Angel holding the Baby in its arms, just moments before He would be held by his earthly mother, Mary. The Heavenly Father, as part of the God Head: God, Jesus and Holy Spirit —had an assignment for His son Jesus. All of creation was moaning from the separation between God and man. Adam and Eve's encounter with Satan in the Garden of Eden had torn mankind apart from their Creator. But the Father had a master plan! Jesus' mission on the earth was to save mankind from themselves and their sins.

All the Heavenly creatures were watching as the mission was launched.
The light of the Father was given to the baby; it was so bright that all of heaven was filled with the glory.
The heavenly orbs —*eclipses 'round about the angel...*
The angel army —*the angel on the right, singing praises...*
The warring, enemy angels —*the angel on the left, its back turned away...* were all present.
And at the bottom, a the sea of humanity watched and waited for their King to arrive.

The battle of Good vs Evil awaited on planet Earth.
The story begins and the final battle waits for Jesus' return.

CHAPTER 10

Kingdom Love

God said, "I love you."

You replied, "Really? How have you loved us?"

"Look at history" (this is God's answer). Malachi 1:1-2

For more than 30 years I have loved glass. Not glass that is milky or cloudy, that you cannot see clearly through, but clear glass without color, without etching, without cuts or cracks. The most expensive pieces of glass are pure and without flaws. My favorite type of glass is just plain clear crystal glass that doesn't distort or distract what lies on the other side. I have given many of these decorative pieces of glass to friends for special occasions such as weddings with a note that says: "Be pure, be true and be transparent with your beliefs." These beautiful pieces of glass remind me of the scriptures:

> *"For now we see through a glass darkly but then face to face: now I know in part, but then shall I know even as also I am known." 1 Corinthians 13:12 (KJ)*

And

"Just as water mirrors your face so your face mirrors your heart."

Proverbs 27:19

I used to wonder when that day would be, when I will be able to see clearly and comprehend God's love for me. I cannot see the face of God directly so I must base my beliefs of God's love on other things. But one day...I will see and I will understand everything he has done to show me his love. I will then know unmistakably that his love motivated everything he did in my life. All I have today, to base that knowledge of his Love on is my history with him and his love stories in his Word. As I study God's Word and the more I know about him, it becomes clear that he has a purpose for all of his actions.

The face of God is not a literal face, but is a spiritual face which is revealed to us a little bit at a time; and yet it's clearer all the time. The pictures of love are knitted in Bible stories and are revealed to my spiritual eyes as I become more aware of and rooted in him through my spiritual growth.

> *"All of us! Nothing between us and God, our faces shining with the brightness of his face. And so we are transfigured much like the Messiah, our lives gradually becoming brighter and more beautiful as God enters our lives and we become like him." 2 Corinthians 3:18*

A limited transformation continues to occur in our spirit; nevertheless, the fullness will not be comprehensive until that day; the day we wake up in the presence of God. The glass and water shared in the scriptures will be so pure and clear, it will be as if nothing separates us from God. There will be no distortions, no flaws. Just as if I am looking through glass or water, God's heart and love will be unveiled, and display his glory. His love will be unmistakably explicit. On earth, God's heart is distorted and only partially understood, but when we stand with him, face to face, we will see him clearly and know him at an entirely new level. These truths have been shared in the Bible, but our minds are limited and cannot comprehend the fullness and completeness of that love. In heaven, we will see all and we will know all of these hidden treasures, just as God knows all that is in our hearts here on earth.

We must look at God with spiritual eyes. God has hidden riches for us in this world. He loves us so much that he sent his Son to save us for eternity and his Holy Spirit to guide us into all truth and reveal the heavenly realm. Both are to express and reveal his love for us. These two aspects of God demonstrate the depth of his love in our personal spiritual life; showing the heart of God through his words and his actions. Seeing clearly then, God's utmost characteristic—kingdom love!

How Does God Demonstrate Love to Us in the Kingdom?

Not only is love demonstrated in the kingdom; but God, himself, is Love and the love of God is the foundation of our faith.

> *"This is how God showed his love for us: God sent his only Son into the world so we might live through him. This is the kind of love we are talking about—not that we once upon a time loved God, but that he loved us and sent his Son as a sacrifice to clear away our sins and damage they've done to our*

relationship with God. My dear, dear friends if God loved us like this, we certainly ought to love each other. No one has seen God, ever. But if we love one another, God dwells deeply within us, and his love becomes complete in us—perfect love! This is how we know we're living steadily and deeply in him, and he in us: He's given us life from his life, from his very own Spirit. Also, we've seen for ourselves and continue to state openly that the Father sent his Son as Savior of the world. Everyone who confesses that Jesus is God's Son participates continuously in an intimate relationship with God. We know it so well, we've embraced it heart and soul, this love that comes from God. GOD is LOVE. When we take up permanent residence in a life of love, we live in God and God lives in us." 1 John 4:9-16

I recognize the power of love in my life as a mother of three wonderful children. Don't misunderstand me, each one of them hasn't always been wonderful. Each has pushed my buttons to points of explosion, but not once was I ever willing to give up my love and support for them. I wish I could say the same about others in my life; however, my love did stay strong and enduring for my children. God's love is even more so for every person that is his child and even those who are not.

"This is how much God loved the world: he gave his Son, his one and only Son. And this is why: so that no one need to be destroyed; by believing in him, anyone can have a whole and lasting life." John 3:16

"God so loved the world, that he gave his Son, Jesus." I am not sure if I could have volunteered any one of my three children for any assignment that would put their lives in jeopardy. (Please God, don't test me!) I just want to be real with you: I'm not sure how God gave Jesus, his son's life up for me, a sinner. For me, it is the truth to say, God's love is much greater than I have the capacity to love in myself. But with God, my ability to love others is able to grow and become stronger and stronger. God's goals, in the area of love, are much bigger and grander than any I could ever comprehend. His goal was to save the world from Satan and create his vision of an earthly kingdom. He loves all of mankind and gives every person a right to make a decision for themselves—to be part of the Kingdom of God or not. If you choose to be part of the Kingdom of God, your capacity for loving even the unlovable will grow to new levels.

A Love Note from God

I remember visiting a Bible school in Alabama for young men with drug and alcohol addictions where my son ministered. I was so amazed by how much love he was giving these young men in need. He would tell me stories of how he had to stay by their side for days while each one fought through the addictive habits that had them in bondage. He shared stories of how he ministered by the Holy Spirit for their deliverance and how he expressed God's love to them. I knew I was lacking in that kind of love. My heart was filled with the joy of seeing my son allow God to work through him to help those guys get free, filled with the Holy Spirit, and turn their lives around. I wanted that same kind of love to flow through me. For over five years, I prayed and thanked God by faith that I would experience his great love in a greater degree. I wanted to love others the way God loves them.

At this time, I was not married and Valentine's Day was always hard to celebrate, as the holiday of love. But, God had a special Valentines gift planned for me. I received a letter in the mail. It changed my life! I opened the envelope and on a beautiful piece of stationary with red roses around the edge, was this letter:

My Child . . .

You may not know *me, but I know everything about you. I know when you sit down and when you rise up. I am familiar with all your ways...* Psalm 139:1-3 *Even the very hairs on your head are numbered...*Matthew 10:29 *For you were made in my image...* Genesis 1:27 *In me you live and move and have your being...*Acts 17:28 *For you are my offspring...*Acts 17:28 *I knew you even before you were conceived...*Jeremiah 1:4-5 *I chose you when I planned creation...*Ephesians 1:11-12 *You were not a mistake...*Psalm 139:15-16 *For all your days are written in my book...*Psalm 139: 15-16 *I determined the exact time of your birth and where you would live...*Acts 17:28 *You are fearfully and wonderfully made...*Psalm 139:14 *I knitted you together in your mother's womb...*Psalm 139:13 *And brought you forth on the day you were born...*Psalm 71:6 *I have been misrepresented by those who don't know me...*John 8:41-44 *I am not distant and angry, but am the complete expression of love...*1 John 4:16 *And it is my desire to lavish my love on you...*1 John 3:1 *Simply because you are my child and I am your Father...*1 John 3:1 *I offer you more than your earthly father ever could...*Matthew 7:11 *For I am the perfect Father...*Matthew 5:48 *Every good gift that you receive comes from my hand...*James 1:17

For I am your provider and I meet all your needs...Matthew 8:31-33 My plans for your future has always been filled with hope...Jeremiah 29:11 Because I love you with an everlasting love...Jeremiah 31:3 My thoughts toward you are as countless as the sand on the seashore...Psalm 139:17-19 And I rejoice over you with singing...Zephaniah 3:17 I will never stop doing good to you...Jeremiah 32:40 For you are my treasured possession...Exodus 19:5 I desire to establish you with all my heart Jeremiah 33:3 If you seek me with all your heart, you will find me...Deuteronomy 4:29 Delight in me and I will give you the desires of your heart...Psalm 37:4 For it is I who gave you those desires...Philippians 2:13 I am able to do more for you than you could possibly imagine...Ephesian 3:20 For I am your greatest encourager...2 Thessalonians 2:15-17 I am also the Father who comforts you in all your troubles...2 Corinthians 1:3-4 When you are brokenhearted, I am close to you...Psalm 34:18 As a shepherd carries a lamb, I have carried you close to my heart...Isaiah 40:11 One day I will wipe away every tear from your eyes...Revelation 21:3-4 And I'll take away all the pain you have suffered on this earth...Revelations 21:4 I am your Father and I love you even as I love my son, Jesus...John 17:23 For in Jesus my love for you is revealed...John 17:26 He is the exact representation of my being...Hebrews 1:3 And he came to demonstrate that I am for you, not against you...Romans 8:31 And to tell you that I am not counting your sins...2 Corinthians 5:18-19 His death was the ultimate expression of my love for you...1 John 4:10 I gave up everything I loved that I might gain your love...Romans 8:32 If you receive the gift of my son Jesus, you receive me...1 John 2:23 And nothing will ever separate you from my love again...Romans 8:38-39 Come home and I'll throw the biggest party heaven has ever seen...Luke 15:7 I have always been Father and will always be Father...Ephesians 3:14-15 My question is...Will you be my child?...John 1:12-13 I am waiting for you...Luke 15:11-32 . . . *Love, Your Dad*

Almighty God

How could I ever question God's love for me again? After all these years, I'm not sure where that letter came from...probably a friend; however, it doesn't matter, God had sent me a special message that Valentine's to remind me of his love for ME. And if he loved me that much, then I would open myself up to loving others as much as he loved me. God will do whatever it takes to get his message to his children. His love note convicted me of truly deep his love is and how it is that love that I must display to others.

I responded with this plea to my Father: "God change me so I can help others through your love." My prayer allowed the Holy Spirit to open doors for me to express God's love to others in my life, which resulted in my character becoming more of a reflection of God's character.

God knows the beginning from the end. He knew man would fall and he planned a way of salvation for all of mankind if they would love him as he loved them.

> *This way, love has the run of the house, becomes at home and mature in us, so that we're free of worry on Judgment Day - our standing in the world is identical with Christ's. There is no room in love for fear. Well-formed love banishes fear. Since fear is crippling, a fearful life—fear of death, fear of judgment—is one not yet fully formed in love. We love him, because he loved us. 1 John 4:17-19*

Because God loves us, we can love others and we will reap the rewards of a life free from fear, free from wondering what the future will be after death and judgment. These fears are just some of the fears non-believers face in tough times if they do not accept God's love for them through his Son, Jesus.

The Gifts God Gave - His Son and His Holy Spirit

The **Love** of God and the **Grace** of our Lord, Jesus Christ, saved us. Not only does God love us but Jesus agreed to be the sacrifice for our salvation. His grace is the glue that holds the "love-plan" together. Jesus' grace gives sinners undeserved acceptance and love—two things which sinners do not deserve. This virtue only comes from God. His divine grace allows the sinner to be the benefactor of salvation; however, there is one other thing needed for the non-believer before he can accept God's plan. The participation of the Holy Spirit to convict the sinner of his need for God in his life. The Holy Spirit continually works with the believer to make that love and grace into an ever-lasting bond between them and the Father God through his Son. It is all joined together into an abiding relationship by the Holy Spirit indwelling man's spirit with his own presence. It takes the three divine persons of God, known as the Trinity, for the complete salvation process of a human soul and then to continue their personal growth through purification and maturing of believers while on earth.

God is love and God is made up of the Trinity; therefore: Father, Son and Holy Ghost are all expressions of this love. Paul said it this way:

> *"The amazing grace of the Master, Jesus Christ, the extravagant love of God (the Father), the intimate friendship of the Holy Spirit, be with all of you." 2 Corinthians 13:14*

The Trinity is the basis for Christian unity in one God; Father, Son and Holy Ghost which is known as the "Spirit" of God.

> *"By means of his one Spirit, we all said good bye to our partial and piecemeal lives. We each used to independently call our own shots, but then we entered into a large and integrated life in which he has the final say in everything. Each of us is now a part of his resurrection body, refreshed and sustained at one fountain—his Spirit—where we all come to drink..." 1 Corinthians 12:13*

We have one hope, made possible by the Lord, Jesus Christ for eternal life. Our Father God has given us the faith we need to accept his salvation, and the Holy Spirit has baptized us into the family of God.

> *"It's in Christ that you, once you heard the truth and believed it* (this is the message of your salvation), *found yourselves home free—signed, sealed, and delivered by the Holy Spirit. The signet from God is the first installment of what's coming, a reminder that we'll get everything God has planned for us, a praising and glorious life." Ephesians 1:13-14*

God used love to put this whole new life together for us. It is God's love that we have been living and training in; it is love that helps us exist, while we fight with our enemy, Satan. It is a love that is beyond any mere words or definitions, or doctrines or denominations.

It is not a love based on head knowledge but a love of the heart that is continually changing and growing as we grow and mature. This love is learned through wisdom, knowledge and understanding, as we experience life on earth. The Bible speaks and tells of the love of God which is revealed through the ministry of the Holy Spirit who reveals it to our spirit. *"It's the mark of God on your heart..." Romans 2:29.*

It is written on the tablets of our hearts and it is the new "kingdom" plan that went in to effect when Jesus died on the cross. It was all expressed to us through God's love...making love the "language" of the Kingdom of God.

> *"The plan wasn't written out with ink on paper, with pages and pages of legal footnotes, killing your spirit. It's written with Spirit on spirit, his life on our lives."* Paul the apostle describes it this way: *"All of us! Nothing between us and God, our faces shining with the brightness of his face. And so we are transfigured much like the Messiah, our lives gradually becoming brighter and more beautiful as God enters our lives and we become like him." 2 Corinthians 3:18*

This new way of life is how we are transformed and display his likeness in us.

Jesus provides righteousness for the believer, along with the promised Holy Spirit, when we accept him as our Savior. What is righteousness? Righteousness allows us the right to have a relationship with God—to be in right standing with him. Sin separated us from that relationship but through Jesus' death on the cross and the shedding of his blood; we have forgiveness and the right to an open relationship with God again. This righteousness is not gained by any words or deeds that we do, but is a righteousness established from our obedient heart which displays the character of God himself. As a result, the "Fruit of the Spirit" begins to develop in the life of the Christian. Note: Righteousness is not optional for a Christian - it is salvation's end product; changing us into right standing with God.

> *"God's kingdom isn't a matter of what you put in your stomach, for goodness' sake. It's what God does with your life as he sets it right, puts it together, and <u>completes it with joy</u>."* *Romans 14:17*

We are not saved by doing righteous things, but by faith in Jesus who provides a way of righteousness through the Holy Spirit. Jesus, after his death on the cross, returned to earth with the keys of hell. With these keys, he controls who enters heaven and hell. For 40 days, Jesus taught his disciples and others what he had accomplished on the cross and gave them one last instruction before he went to his home in heaven.

> *"...until the day he said good-bye to the apostles, the ones he had chosen through the Holy Spirit, and was taken up to heaven after his death, he*

> *presented himself alive to them in many different settings over a period of forty days. In the face-to-face meetings, he talked to them about things concerning the kingdom of God. As they met and ate meals together, he told them that they were on NO account to leave Jerusalem but MUST WAIT FOR THE FATHER'S PROMISE: THE PROMISE YOU HEARD FROM ME.* (Caps for emphasis) *John baptized in water, you will be baptized in the Holy Spirit. And soon." Acts 1:2-5*

The Apostle Luke also wrote about Jesus' declaration:

> *"You're the first to hear and see it. You're the witnesses. What comes next is very important: I am sending what my Father promised to you, so stay here in the city until he arrives, until you're equipped with power from on high." Luke 24:48-49*

What was the promise? It was the promise of the Holy Spirit and that he would produce "*righteousness, joy and peace*". These attributes are the result of the Holy Spirit living and ministering to those who have been saved by believing in Jesus. The Holy Spirit, together with the Word of God, produces fruit in us. This results in quality living in the kingdom. It results in the renewing of our minds into a mind that thinks like God thinks. How does this happen?

- The fruit that is produced has a seed in it that reproduces. That seed is planted in our mind and spirit.
- As we study the Word of God, we are watering that seed so that it has the nutrients to grow and multiply in us.
- The Holy Spirit guides us in the truth and deeper meanings of the Word which results in our desire for more of its truth.
- The seed combines with the continual watering of the Word.
- It grows and the mind starts to think as God thinks.
- The renewed mind helps us to determine God's will for us and what pleases him.

The renewed mind through the Holy Spirit confirms that love must rule over everything we do. And it is through this renewed mind, that the Holy Spirit will teach us how to love others like we love ourselves. To do this, we must be filled with the knowledge of God's will by means of the Holy Spirit's wisdom and knowledge developing in us. How do we do this?

> *"So here's what I want you to do. God helping you. Take your everyday, ordinary life—sleeping, eating, going-to-work, and walking around-life—and place it before God as an offering. Embracing what God does for you is the best thing you can do for him. Don't become so well-adjusted to your culture that you fit into it without even thinking. Instead, fix your attention on God. You'll be changed from the inside out. Readily recognize what he wants from you, and quickly respond to it. Unlike the culture around you, always dragging you down to its level of immaturity, God brings the best out of you, develops well-informed maturity in you." Roman 12:1-2*

The Results of Walking in the Spirit

Our job as a believer is not to fulfill the desires of the flesh, but fulfilling the desires of God by living a righteous life. A righteous life means to "walk in the spirit", exhibiting a changed behavior of walking in love.

> *"Watch what God does, and then you do it, like children who learn proper behavior from their parents. Mostly what God does is love you. Keep company with him and learn a life of love. Observe how Christ loved us. His love was not cautious but extravagant. He didn't love in order to get something from us but to give everything of himself to us. Love like that. Don't allow love to turn into lust...gossip...religion...smooth talk...will get you nowhere, certainly nowhere near the kingdom of Christ, the kingdom of God." Ephesians 5:1-5*

To walk in the Spirit is to walk in freedom; not in "bondage of the world", by thinking you can do whatever you want. Instead use your freedom to serve one another in love; that's how freedom grows.

> *"For everything we know about God's Word is summed up in a single sentence: Love others as you love yourself." Galatians 5:14*

Love in action is freedom. Acting in self-interest instead of love is incompatible with the God-kind of love and walking in the spirit. Jesus has set us free to live a free life. Be cautious and don't allow legalism to creep back into your Christian walk. Legalistic religion returns us to bondage and takes us out of the love-walk. If we attempt to revert back to our own religious plans, we are cut off from Christ Jesus because of sin; this causes us to fall out of grace. Then the only way to regain our justification and righteousness is by confessing the sin and asking for forgiveness; allowing us to walk in the spirit of love again. The more we walk in God's love, the more we will display his character. God's character can be seen in the 9 Fruits of the Spirit (Galatians 5:22-23). These qualities are what we should strive to display in our daily life in his kingdom:

1. **Love** -This word captures the essence of God's character in his relationship to his own people. It is expressed through God sending his Son to die for our eternal relationship with the Father.
2. **Joy** – is God's expression of giving us a full pardon for our sins and allowing us to walking in the Spirit. Because of our joy, we cry "ABBA" (a word for "father" that Jesus used to express his own intimate relationship with God). This causes unquenchable, uninhibited joy as believers await the hope of righteousness and appreciate the joy only found in Jesus' salvation.
3. **Peace** – God himself is described as "the God of peace", who dwells in total shalom (wholeness, well-being) and who gives shalom to his people. Through him we keep the unity of the Spirit in the bond of peace. (Ephesians 4:3)
4. **Patience** – God is patient with us and we need to be patient with others. This is God's love in action toward us. Being patient requires us to "put on" godly attitudes when facing those who stand against us. It requires us to stand in love with others who need long-suffering and patience instead of outbursts of rage toward them.
5. **Kindness** – A godly action to display patience toward others by showing love. God's kindness is found in his actions of mercy toward people who deserve his wrath. This is expressed through God's grace toward us in Christ.
6. **Goodness** – is closely allied with kindness. It is a more all-embracing quality which is displayed in believers as "full of goodness". Therefore, this characteristic of Christian grace is produced in the life of a believer by the Spirit. Those who walk in the Spirit, walk in doing "good" to all.

7. **Faith** - or faithfulness is God's characteristic of always being faithful to us no matter how we disappoint him. He is faithful to us, therefore, our life should show faithful living because we trust in God over the long haul. Believers should express faithfulness toward others by showing all the "fruit of the Spirit", as God shows it to us.
8. **Gentleness** – is also translated as "meekness". It conveys the sense of humility toward God and others and is expressed in believers who walk by the Spirit to restore others who are consumed in sin. By recognizing our own faults, we walk in humility and do not think ourselves better than others.
9. **Self-Control** – is learning to live a life of moderation instead of excess. It is the only virtue which is aimed at the individual believer. It is aimed at indulgences of the flesh (sexual immorality, impurity, debauchery and other excesses such as drunkenness, over-eating, etc.) Only the Spirit can set us free with a life of moderation; no longer out of control.

When my children were little, I taught the fruit of the Spirit through songs. (Agape Land's Music Machine - Fruit of the Spirit). It was a great way for them to learn what God expects of us. These songs planted the seeds of the fruit of the Spirit in the subconscious of my family; helping each of us to understand and grow the fruit in our lives. This helped to define the sub-culture of our family unit. All of us today find ourselves singing parts of the songs when we get tested in these areas.

One of the best Scriptures for showing us how to put the fruit of the Spirit in action in our lives is Romans 12:3-21. These are examples of the fruit of the Spirit helping us live successfully in the Kingdom of God. (I have added the name of the fruit it represents at the end of each statement to help you see that all nine of the "Fruit of the Spirit" are acknowledged!)

> *"I'm speaking to you out of deep gratitude for all that God has given me* (Paul)... *Living then, as every one of you does, in pure grace* (un-merited favor with God), *it's important that you not misinterpret yourselves as people who are bringing this goodness to God. No, God brings it all to you. The only accurate way to understand ourselves is by what God is and by what he does for us, not by what we are and what we do for him...*
>
> - *Don't burn out, keep yourselves fueled and aflame.* **SELF-CONTROL**
> - *Be alert servants of the Master cheerfully expectant.* **JOY**

- *Don't quit in hard times; pray all the harder.* **FAITH**
- *Help needy Christians, be inventive in hospitality.* **KINDNESS**
- *Bless your enemies, no cursing under your breath.* **PEACE**
- *Laugh with your happy friends when they're happy, share tears when they're down.* **GENTLENESS**
- *Get along with each other, don't be stuck up. Make friends with nobodies, don't be the great somebody.* **LOVE & GENTLENESS**
- *Don't hit back; discover beauty in everyone. If you've got it in you, get along with everybody. Don't insist on getting even; that's not for you to do. "I'll do the judging," says God. "I'll take care of it."* **SELF-CONTROL & GOODNESS**
- *Our Scriptures tell us that if you see your enemy hungry, go buy that person lunch, or if he's thirsty, get him a drink. Your generosity will surprise him with goodness.* **GOODNESS**
- *Don't let evil get the best of you; get the best of evil by going good."* **PATIENCE & FAITH** *Roman 12:3-21*

The Holy Spirit was given to us to be our helper and to produce the "Fruit of the Spirit" in our lives. The Holy Spirit produces in us God's righteous character, so that we can reflect his likeness to others. Without the Spirit to help us display these characteristics, we cannot grow in his likeness and move from glory to glory in him. All of this was designed by God to show his love to us. He loved us enough to give his son so that we would be able to have everlasting life with him in heaven and God gave us the Holy Spirit, so we could live a life of purpose and love where we could grow into maturity and fulfill our destiny here on earth.

Ways to Access the Glory Given to Us

The love of God was shown at the cross and foundationally finished at the cross and its purpose was to engage us into kingdom life. And as we have studied the many aspects of the kingdom life in this book, we should discover the kingdom is the door to the glory realm for the believer. Now we realize that the greatest manifestation of God's glory is the undeserved love he gives us. This love frees us to live in his likeness and walk in his Spirit. God knew man would break his blood covenant established at creation; and therefore, God cut a new covenant through Jesus, who left his "God title" in heaven and came to earth as a man with all the charactistics of man. As a result of Jesus' actions on earth, man is able to reclaim what he had lost in the beginning when Adam sinned. Jesus was the perfect man without sin. He proved that we could live a godly life on earth. God was faithful to his plan and never aborted what he knew man could not do himself, save his relationship with God. Today, we have all of God's promises as a result of our relationship with Jesus and his willingness to shed his blood for our sins. With that relationship, God's glory manifests itself in kingdom benefits.

Typically on the earth, mortal man seeks his own glory, but as Christians in the Kingdom of God, humans can have the same heavenly glory that Father God gave Jesus.

> *"He* (God) *thought of everything, provided for everything we could possibly need, letting us in on the plans he took such delight in making. He set it all out before us in Christ, a long-range plan in which everything would be brought together and summed up in him, everything in deepest heaven, and everything on planet earth. It's in Christ that we find out what we are and what we are living for...I asked the God of our Master, Jesus Christ, the God of glory—to make you intelligent and discerning in knowing him personally, your eyes focused and clear, so that you can see exactly what it is he is calling you to do, grasp the immensity of his glorious way of life he has for Christians..." Ephesians 1:8-10, 17-18*

So, if Jesus gave us the same glory, it would be wise if we knew how to access the glory to make a difference in how we see ourselves and others in the Kingdom of God here on earth.

- <u>Strive to be a true disciple of Jesus</u> – Jesus gave his glory to the disciples. So we must strive to be a disciple and function as his 12 disciples did. These 12 men sat at the feet of their Lord which gave them favor for all of eternity. They showed us how to live as a disciple:
  1) Be a follower—they were determined to forsake everything and everyone to follow Jesus. Be willing to do God's will in your life.
  2) Be a student—they sat at Jesus' feet and listened to him teach. We must stay in the Word of God and listen to the guidance of the Holy Spirit. Study to show yourself approved.

3) Be a servant—they did whatever Jesus asked them to do, even when tired or weary. They fed the multitudes and went from one gathering to another. They always went the extra mile to serve Jesus. We can feed the hungry and serve our pastors and missionaries as well as feed and serve the needy and lost souls of the world.

- Climb your personal mountain to be with the Lord.
    1) Jesus and Moses both accessed God's glory on mountains. Jesus on the Mountain of Transfiguration and Moses on Mount. Sinai. They both went to the mountain to be in Father's presence and commune with him. It was on these two mountains that they both experienced the glory of God.
    2) Both left their place of comfort to spend time alone with God. Make a special effort to be with him and ask to see his glory. By being with him, we can learn to think his thoughts and feel his emotions. What a privilege!
- Be humble and full of love—both of these qualities are learned and experienced by being in God's presence and willing to let the Holy Spirit grow us into Jesus' likeness. *"And what God gives in love is far better than anything else you'll find. It's common knowledge that 'God goes against the willful proud; God gives grace to the willing humble.'" James 4:6*
    1) Pride comes naturally, but being humble takes effort. When you are humble, you will get extra grace.
    2) We usually don't love the unlovable, but by making a decision to love our enemies, you make a choice resulting in the grace needed to love more.

By striving to submit to Jesus we are opening ourselves to experience more of his glory. At the same time, the Holy Spirit is growing the Fruit of the Spirit in us and helping us to change and move from "Glory to Glory" in him.

The kingdom is a unique place. It is both internal and external in our lives; both inside in our hearts and outside in our actions of love to others. We need spiritual eyes to see it. *"Your eyes focused and clear, so that you can see exactly what it is he is calling you to do, grasp the immensity of this glorious way of life he has for Christians, oh, the utter extravagance of his work in us who trust him—endless energy, boundless strength!"* Jesus said the Kingdom of God is in your midst and it is in your heart! (Luke 17:20-21)

CONCLUSION—we experience God's Love and then we give it away to others. When we love we are obeying one of God's greatest commands. "If you love me, love others as you love yourself." John 13:34

"One day soon we will all see through the glass clearly"

Until then we are in the process of being refined into God's image.

God's gave two gifts of Love
His Son
And
The Holy Spirit

How fluent are you in the kingdom's love language?

What is next...

Seek First His Kingdom of Righteousness and Its Blessings!

God had a plan from the very beginning – to set up a kingdom on earth known as the Kingdom of God. The plan was derailed by Satan in the Garden of Eden; but, God had a default plan. It included utilizing every resource he had to show the "corrupted world" how much he loved it and how much he was willing to give to set-up his kingdom on earth.

God has given man over 2000 years to establish God's kingdom on the earth through his believers. Man had the benefit of utilizing the inspired Word of God and the Holy Spirit to accomplish it. Each of us has that power when we get saved to make our individual life a "heaven on earth" experience by building the Kingdom of God in our heart. However, many of Jesus' believers have not been willing to submit to God's way. God's way requires man to submit his own will to God's will.

Without man's submission to the will of God, believers have been unsuccessful in restoring the earth to its original perfect condition as God had planned. So God has another plan ready to launch to set the earth back on course again! The Apostle John wrote about the future of God's kingdom on earth in Revelation. It is our responsibility as believers to be prepared for the future and Jesus' continual rule over the earth.

> Paul told us to... *"ask the God of our Master, Jesus Christ, the God of glory—to make you* (believers) *intelligent and discerning in knowing him* (Jesus) *personally, your eyes focused and clear, so that you can see exactly what it is he is calling you to do, grasp the immensity of this glorious way of life he has for Christians, all this energy issues from Christ: God raised him from death and set him on a throne in deep heaven in charge of running the universe, everything from galaxies to governments, no name and power exempt from his rule. And not just for the time being, but forever."* Ephesians 1:17-18

Jesus' plan includes the Church Age that we are presently a part of, as well as the Millennial Age, which is to come. In the millennium, Jesus will return to earth for 1,000 years. Paul prayed that the eyes of our heart, our spiritual eyes, would be opened to see the future kingdom. God has set Jesus in complete authority to rule the universe including the earth for all eternity. No one knows what the complete picture of eternity will look like, but we do know what is coming next in Jesus' Kingdom of God.

It would take another book to write in depth about the end times leading up to this future millennial age, which is not the purpose of this book. However, if we do not discuss where we are heading, this book on kingdom principles would not be complete.

Jesus describes the coming signs of the end of this age as a world of increasing discord and chaos but the Christians of his kingdom will experience a place of increasing peace and joy. How does that happen, while the world is falling apart, that believers will have increasing joy and peace?

> *"God's kingdom...is righteousness and peace, and joy in the Holy Ghost. Your task is to single-mindedly serve Christ. Do that and you'll kill two birds with one stone: pleasing the God above you and proving your worth to the people around you." Romans 14:17-18*

This is the contrast that is happening in the Kingdom of God today. As the world grows in fear and depression, we as Christians grow in peace and joy. By us doing what is right in Jesus' sight, we become more righteous, enjoying more of his blessings of peace and joy, yet the world falls into deeper crisis causing fear to be magnified. Jesus said, *"I've told you all this so that trusting me, you will be unshakable and assured, deeply at peace. In this godless world you will continue to experience difficulties. But take heart! I've conquered the world." John 16:33*

Do you want to experience tribulation which brings fear or do you want to build your life on Jesus' kingdom principles and have peace and joy?

Seek ye first the Kingdom of God, and his righteousness,

And all these things shall be added unto you. Matthew 6:33 KJ

Birth Pains

1971 was a life-changing year for me. My husband and I left Texas and moved to California for his job, I had my first child 1 week before the move, and I discovered Hal Lindsey's book, The Late Great Planet Earth. All of these things shook my life but the longest lasting change was Hal Lindsey's book. From that time to now, I have continually been interested in the return of the Lord Jesus to the earth and the tribulation period that is foretold in Revelation. All of my family think I am a little crazy because I have been watching everything that happens in the world and somehow try to relate it to the end time prophesies talked about in the Bible. Time after time they've just laughed at me and said, "Mom, people from the beginning of time have said this is the end of the world but they were wrong and we are still here." I just want to say that I am not obsessed about the end time, but I will always be watching for Jesus' return.

In Matthew 25 verses 1-13, Jesus tells the story of the ten young virgins (the Christians of the church age) who were waiting for the bridegroom (Jesus) to get married (the rapture of the church age believers). Five of the virgins were ready when he came to get them with full lamps of oil and they were immediately taken into the wedding supper. But the other five foolish virgins did not have enough oil and had to go buy more. After they purchased more oil and went to the bridegroom, he did not let them in to the supper and said he didn't even know them. Why did he refuse them entrance? They had not been prepared and ready. I want to be one of the first five virgins who are ready for Jesus' return—I don't want to just say I am ready but I want to be ready! That means to be a dedicated follower of Jesus and the Bible—and actively working to grow in wisdom and knowledge of his Word. So one area of my biblical studies has been "End Time Prophecy".

Jesus and other apostles taught many times on the signs of Jesus' second coming. So, we must look at it too. God's kingdom plan will continually move forward and it will include the Rapture of Believers and Jesus' Second Coming and the establishment of a new earth in the Millennium Age.

Jesus in his teachings said these signs are the birth pains of the end of the present age:

- There will be many deceivers and false messiahs who will lead people astray (these deceivers will try to lead even the elect astray). Luke 4 and Isaiah 61
- There will be wars and rumors of war (to date we have had over 15,000 wars since Jesus stated this). Luke 4 and Isaiah 61
- The Jewish people would re-gather back into the land of Israel. (The establishment of Israel as a nation in 1948 is considered a Super Sign). Ezekiel 37
- The rise of Russia as a superpower in the 1950's and re-establishment as a military state today will lead to its destruction. Ezekiel 38-39
- The rise of Capitalism and labor conflicts. James 5:1-6
- An increase in travel and knowledge. Daniel 12:4
- Apostasy and Occultism where people give up their faith and chase after the demonic. 2 Timothy 4:1-2
- Moral breakdown of society. 2 Peter 3:1-12
- One-World Church. Revelation 17
- One-World Government. Daniel 2

Let's look at what Jesus said when the disciples questioned him, giving them clues about when the end would be.

> *"Watch out for the doomsday deceivers. Many leaders are going to show up with forged identities claiming, 'I'm the one,' or 'The end is near.' Don't fall for any of that. When you hear of wars and uprisings, keep your head and don't panic. This is routine history and no sign of the end."* He went on,

> *"Nations will fight nation and ruler fight rulers, over and over. Famines and earthquakes will occur in various places. This is nothing compared to what is coming." Matthew 24:4-9*

In past times, we have seen many people claiming to be the Messiah and there have been thousands of wars over the centuries but the end has not come. These things must be coupled with lots of other signs too. No one sign in itself pronounces the end is near. It is the increase of the signs and the combinations of all the signs that is a clear signal that the end is coming. Let's look at today's signs.

We are now seeing an increase in earthquakes and famines. Since the turn of the 21st century, we have had massive earthquakes that have rocked our planet and caused it to wobble on its axis. The South Asian tsunami hit nine nations and killed 250,000 people. Another earthquake devastated Pakistan and killed 80,000 people. Shortly thereafter, earthquakes in Chile, New Zealand, Haiti, and Nepal killed another 250,000 people and left millions grieving, homeless and starving from famine. Then the enormous 9.0 quake hit Japan, killing thousands more and caused the nuclear meltdown and widespread poisoning caused by leakage of radioactive contamination. We continually see earthquakes happening in areas of the world which are not known for this type of activity. More are predicted but where and when is only known by God.

Another sign of the end times is nations having food shortages and man is diligently working to solve this problem. Monsanto is exploring the alteration of natural seed to make "super" seeds that make 100 times as much food when planted and nurtured correctly. Is it God's way, to alter nature and the seed that he provided for the replenishment of the earth?

Jesus also told us to watch for signs in the heavens. Cosmic events are being seen in the heavenly realm and comets are coming unusually close to earth. In February 2013, Russia was rocked by a meteorite explosion where large numbers of people were hospitalized and buildings were damaged. Numerous other meteors have hit uninhabited locations on the earth.

Yes, there are signs God is showing us that end times could be near and these signs will continue to increase until Jesus returns. God will use these signs and disasters to bring men to himself and give everyone the opportunity to accept Jesus as their Savior. God tells man to watch and be prepared for Jesus' return. No one knows the day or time when Jesus will rapture his church to be with him and then afterward return to earth with his believers to rebuild the perfect earth as God intended it be. But we must be ready, watching and willing to do God's will so that we won't be like the foolish virgins and miss Jesus' timing. Jesus said in Matthew,

> *"Stay with it—that's what God requires. Stay with it to the end. You won't be sorry and you'll be saved. All during this time, the good news—the Message of the kingdom—will be preached all over the world, a witness staked out in every country. And then the end will come." Matthew 24:13-14*

You see I'm not a dooms-day person, but I am a realistic Christian who wants to be ready for what is next in God's plan. To be ready, we must be aware of where we are in God's timing.

While watching for the signs of Jesus return, his followers should be continually seeking the Kingdom of God and his righteousness. All should continually be growing and maturing in their character, to be more like God by walking in love while praising and worshiping him for all he has provided in his kingdom.

God's "love plan" is manifested through these coming events. He wishes for all to be saved and turn over their life to him and live by his principles. He is giving every person the opportunity to accept his love and to grow in the kingdom principle of LOVE. He wants us to share his plan with every person on the earth so they will have the opportunity to accept all he has for them, not only now but through the coming days in the Millennium Age. Our job is to give his love to others. Are you sharing his love with others that enter your sphere of influence?

Are you ready for your King, Jesus, to return to earth for his church? Today's Kingdom of God is our training ground for eternity. Cross over to the life God has planned for you and be prepared. The Bible says that God knew us before we were born and he has a destiny for each one, personally. Are you seeking your part of the plan...your destiny? Now is the time - the future is closer than you think!

Be sure to read the Epilogue, which explains
*the vision in **Chapter 1 - God's Plan for Us**.*

Kingdom Thinking

What did God mean in Malachi 1:2, when he said if you want to know how he has loved us, look at history?

Give two ways you know that God's love is real to YOU?

Since we can't see God with our physical eyes, how do you see him and his glory in your life?

What was God's ultimate sacrifice to show his love for us? Do you agree that your answer is to you the ultimate sacrifice? Why?

Define “grace”. How does grace allow us to be saved for eternity?

The Holy Spirit will produce what three characteristics in Christian believers’ lives?

Explain how the 9 fruits of the spirit are produced in our life.

When you quote Jesus saying, *"Seek ye first the Kingdom of God, and his righteousness, and all these things shall be added unto you." (Matthew 6:33 KJ);* what are "these things" to you?

What does God mean when he talks about the birth pains of the future? Many people today are walking in fear when they see the signs of the end times. What is God's purpose for these signs?

Are You and your family ready for the Return of Jesus? What needs to happen for you to get ready and what do you need to do for your family to be ready?

Keys to the Kingdom

- God is love and his love is continually being revealed to us as we grow in knowledge of who he is. Only in heaven will we see the finished product of his love for us.
- God is motivated by love and he says his greatest commandment is to "love others as we love ourselves".
- We are a reflection to those around us of who God is. As we grow in understanding God's love and walk in it, that reflection is constantly shining brighter and brighter to others.
- Where there is love, fear is banished.
- Righteousness is salvation's end product and our greatest benefit in the kingdom is that through righteousness we have a relationship with God.
- When we walk in righteousness and grace, we produce the fruit of the Spirit in our life, resulting in our ability to please God by walking in the Spirit.
- The 12 disciples demonstrated a life of walking in the Spirit. They are great examples of how we should display God's love to others by being 1) a follower of Jesus, 2) a student of Jesus' teachings, and 3) a servant to Jesus and others.
- The kingdom of God is in your heart (spirit).
- To enjoy ALL the benefits of kingdom life, we must put God and his will first in our lives.

Be sure to read the Epilogue, which explains the vision in ***Chapter 1 - God's Plan for Us.***

Epilogue

God's plan for you requires his perfect alignment of all things in order for you to reach your destiny. But reaching the target is dependent on one important thing - you being willing to do your part and get aligned with his plan!

The Vision's Interpretation—Our Destiny

The stage is set with me sitting in my car, enjoying what seems like a lovely drive on a beautiful sunny spring day, only to realize that I was actually waiting patiently for God to launch me into a new season of my life. In the past, it seemed like God was not in any rush to make things happen, so I had repetitiously tried to make it happen my way. I was now tired of trying to burst my cocoon myself and I was ready to let God do it his way. When I finally released myself to God, I realized that things around me were being prepared for a change. Lights (representing hope of what the future might have for me) are turned on as the preparations are made for the journey. My renewed hope was now turning into faith, and I can see that everything in my past was allowed to happen in order to prepare me for God's plan. At this point, I know, without a doubt, that I love God and I am now ready to do God's perfect will for my life. The atmosphere is charged with excitement for what will happen next. I am no longer full of fear and anxiety, instead allowing God's grace to release love, joy and peace to flow and fill my spirit.

When I least expected something to happen...all of a sudden God was moving in ways that I would not have anticipated. A door opened from heaven which allowed powerful winds of the Spirit of God to enter around me. Unseen objects are being modified for a launch into the unknown area before me. I could hear cracking sounds as other things were aligned for what would happen next. Preparations didn't slow down but continued to speed up, but nothing seemed to be affecting me personally. I couldn't help but wonder what all was going on; however, I knew all the activity was a result of my submission to God, allowing him to set the stage for the coming event. I knew everything was being prepared for me.

Knowing God's Word, I knew God was preparing everything I would need to accomplish his goals in my life. He is always working behind the scenes to make sure everything is available: the materials, tools and provisions I would need to not just survive, but to prosper. God does not take the preparation stage lightly. Not his part nor mine; both must be in place before he allows any of his children to begin the journey he has for them. My part is to activate my faith and to trust him to help me along the way. It is in the moments before the action starts that I must be doing my job to prepare for the journey too. It is this time that I am to plant his Word deep in my spirit, show God my determination to follow him and allow his Holy Spirit to strengthen my spirit.

Even with the activities that have been required for the preparation, I still know I could be on the edge of disaster if I don't keep God first in my thoughts and actions. Just for a moment, my thoughts rush to unexpected images of destruction. The wind reminds me of the roar of the enemy trying to fill me with fear. I must fight through the battle in my mind and not let fear overwhelm me. I look around me and realize I am in a protected place and peace fills my soul again. God has prepared me for this time and this job. He has an army of angels around me and the Holy Spirit is whispering in my ear, reassuring me of who I am in Christ. He is reassuring me and asking me to draw near to him, listen to his still small voice, and ask him for the faith I need to complete what he has started for me.

The "God of the Angel Army" is with me and he has the fighting forces, equipment and supplies needed for any battle I will face on my assigned journey. I am confident God is with me as I stand at a gate I must go through to conquer my promise land. This is the time that God has called me to, prepared me for and promised me many years ago would be my destiny.

As I survey the area and look ahead to the future, God is standing just behind me and gives me a gentle push causing me to take my first step. At first, it was as if I had lost all control of everything around me. It seemed as if no matter whether I tried to go left or right, fast or slow…I was being magnetically drawn to a target. The forces around me were stronger than I was. My mind told me I was out of control, but my spirit knew that something bigger than me was directing the course I was to follow. I knew in my spirit that it was God. And his target was my destiny!

God is definitely in control and his desire is that I will trust him no matter what might happen. Without seeing the entire plan, it would be easy for me to try to get back in the driver's seat and take control again. So God tests me to see if I am as committed to him as he is committed to me. He pushes me again, just a little. I now realize I am at a new crossing over in my life. In his wisdom, he reassured me that he is there for me. I lay back and rest, knowing I'm in his will and in his plan until finally I'm at complete peace waiting to experience the next step.

All of a sudden, things start to intensify and I sense that a trigger has been pulled and all the rest and refreshing I have had was to prepare me for the final dash to reach the target. I can look back and see that everything so far has brought me to this exact moment in time. God opens my eyes and my ears to new levels of awareness so I can see and hear his directions. He once again speaks into my spirit that all I need to do is what he tells me to do. He gently says, "stay close to ME and follow my instructions and all will be fine." The environment around me seems to be under siege and lots of confusion is developing. I start to get anxious, but he comforts me again and says "stay in my will".

My cocoon now seems to be a time capsule speeding toward the target yet at the same time, allowing me to experience excitement with the confidence I am doing what God expects of me. I feel as if nothing can stop me from my destiny. At any moment, I could take things back in my control, to analyze what I could do to ensure all goes well; but if I do, I realize, I put God's plan in jeopardy. I must wait patiently; rest in God, knowing that I am experiencing his love and his plan for me. I will not disappoint my God at this important time. I will do "God's will" not mine; each step of the way.

I have learned many things can derail God's plans. Yet, our God is flexible and he doesn't stop helping me get to my destiny if things go differently than expected. Mankind's destinies are woven together and it takes all of us to make it happen. When I am the cause of missed timing, it affects not only my destiny but it can affect hundreds of others' destiny too. This doesn't stop God; He will just start re-aligning circumstances again to put us back on track to all of our targeted destinies.

At the last moment, something unplanned can occur. But was it unexpected to God? No, God knows the entire plan of my life. He has a plan for each of his children and he knows all the things that could go wrong. And, God will redeem the time to restructure my life to get me to my destiny. He will use everything in my life for his purpose to mature and grow me into the person he saw me to be before I was born. He will restructure everything around me to get me realigned again in his kingdom on earth to accomplish my destiny. My job is to use the principles of his kingdom, to enjoy the benefits he provides, and to stay in his will, until that destiny is completed. Aligning ourselves with God directs us toward that goal, but God has the big picture in his plan and when I miss my target through my own fault or that of another, God will re-align the rest of the universe for his purpose and our destiny. When we are at our weakest and have nowhere to turn, we must become dependent on him to re-align us. Our dependence on him is one of his greatest tests and allows him to show us one of his highest kingdom principles: that when we are weak, he is strong.

We must stay focused on what is ahead and not look back, yet be in the present and appreciate that God is able to open every door for us, at just the right time so we can walk into our destiny with joy and confidence. He is with us, continuing to providing all we need—physical strength, finances and alignment.

His kingdom is based on each of his children doing "his will". Will you commit to God anew, to do his will in your life? Will you stay in God's will so you can see how your destiny unfolds to meet the need of his unified destiny?

That is kingdom life at its best.

That is "A Joy Filled Life!"

A Glimpse of Destiny

by Joy E. Miller

"A Glimpse of Destiny" was painted to reminds us that we do not always have a complete picture of what our destiny will be; but, if we continue to do God's will, we will always be headed in the right direction. Along the way, we will get small glimpses of ours, from time to time, as we walk God's narrow path along the way.

Glorious God, I celebrate the fact that my eyes have never seen, my ears have never heard, and my mind has never conceived what you have prepared for me and all the others who truly love you. Help me to understand that this awesome plan is revealed to me by Your Spirit.

Based on Corinthians 2:9

Bibliography

Allison, L. (2009). *Kingdom Alignment.* Peoria, Arizona: Intermedia Publishing Group, Inc.

Brim, B. (1995). *The Blood and The Glory.* Colllnsville, Oklahoma: Harrison House, Inc.

Brown, F. (1062). A Hebrew and English Lexicon of the Old Testament. Oxford, London, New York .

Capps, C. (1980). *Authority in Three Worlds.* Tulsa, Oklahoma: Harrison House, Inc. Retrieved from ISBN 0-89274-281-X

Fee, G. D. (1996). In *Paul, the Spirit, and the People of God.* Peabody, Massachuetts: Hendrickson Publishers Inc.

Huch, L. (2000). Breaking the Cycle of Family Curses, FREE at LAST. Portland, Oregon: Albury Publishing. Retrieved from ISBN 1-5778-124-4

Jackson, J. P. (1999). *Needless Casualties of War.* Flower Mound, Texas, Texas: Streams Books. Retrieved from ISBN 158483-000-X

Wigglesworth, S. (1998). *Smith Wiggleswoth on the Holy Spirit* (Vol. 1). (G. G.-A. Archives, Ed.) Springfield, , Missouri, United States of America: Whitaker House. Retrieved from ISBN 0-88368-544-2

Special Acknowledgments

Thanks to teachers and friends in my life that have taken the time to share and mentor me along the way.

- Lora Allison, Mary Bostram, and Susan Harris have been long term spiritual friends who have help me make this journey. Rachel Harris, my friend and editor, who diligently helped many hours with drafts and re-writes.
- Danny Lee Smothermon, my son and pastor, who has always believed in my abilities and has been a constant encourager that God is not finished with me yet.
- And of course, my Heavenly Father who has always showed me his patience, grace and love to see this to completion.

Follow Joy as she continues her "Journey to DESTINY"
Visit blog.ajoyfilledlife.org

To see more of Joy's paintings in color, order art prints and copies of her books,
visit www.ajoyfilledlife.org

Joy is also available for teaching and speaking engagements and special events.
Send inquiries to joymiller@ajoyfilledlife.org

www.ingramcontent.com/pod-product-compliance
Lightning Source LLC
Chambersburg PA
CBHW062040090426
42740CB00016B/2965

* 9 7 8 0 9 9 6 8 7 1 5 6 3 *